THE JYOTIRLING

HUMAN FAITH REDEFINED

DEBABRATA MAULIK

RIGI PUBLICATION

All right reserved

No part of this book may be reproduced in any form, by photostat, microfilm, xerography, or any other means or incorporated into any information retrieval system, electronic or mechanical, without the written permission of the copyright owner.

THE JYOTIRLING

HUMAN FAITH REDEFINED

By

DEBABRATA MAULIK

Copyright© DEBABRATA MAULIK 2021

Originally published in India

Edition: 1

ISBN: 978-81-948315-4-9

Printer: Manipal Printers

Published by RIGI PUBLICATION

777, Street no.9, Krishna Nagar Khanna-141401 (Punjab), India

Website: www.rigipublication.com

Email: info@rigipublication.com

Phone: +91-9357710014, +91-9465468291

His Abode on the Earth

If he were not there to help God Somdev (Moon) we would have deprived from Moonlight. If he did not save the people of Ujjain from the oppressor we would not have the present day Ujjain city. River Narmada would not have been worshipped if he did not appear there at Omkar, Mandhata. He saved the mankind by rescuing his disciples from the oppressor King at Darukavana. It is his blessings at Setubandh which helped Ayodhya Prince Rama to get rid of tormenter King Ravana. If he was not there at Tryambak, Sage Gautam would not have lived and flow of human race would have hampered. At Verul village his kind appearance saved his disciples and saved mankind. It is he who fought a valiant battle with devil Bhima at Khed taluka to save God Vishnu. It is he who appeared in one of the most difficult terrains of Nallamala mountain range to save the Chenchu tribes. Providence brought him to Deoghar to nurse suffering mankind when arrogant King Ravana was on his way back to Lanka. It is he who rescued the fratricide Pandava brothers from their sin and saved the mankind. All these mythological events are centered on magnanimous Lord Shiva, the Master of the Universe. His "Swayambhu" appearance in all these incidences created Jyotirling Shrines, the abode of Lord Shiva.

Author's Comments

"The way we live, we dress and we appear stand to identify us with our custom and practices as relevant environment demands, while the attitude of high handedness and chronic arrogance make out one with the follower of fiend. Humanity by its nature never compromise with the basic principle of righteousness. Those who evade this humanitarian call stand to perish by the call of the Kaal (Time)"

Reminisce brings back my childhood days vividly before me. As a boy I used to be a regular visitor of folk arts. The Performing Folk Artists used to discourse tales from our Epic the Ramayana. The theatrical act of the narrator mixed with background music in step with his recital influenced my infancy mind. His acts used to glue the audience to the episodes of the Epic narrated for an hour each day. The program used to continue for a month. My involvement with mythological characters set off in my mind. My childhood inquisitiveness used to make me wonder about the Mythology. Subsequent anecdote of life shifted priorities over the next few decades of adulthood. Reality of life forced temporary fading of those inquisitives. In my retired days these prying came back. It shook me from within. Keen urges motivated me to pursue these faded curiosity.

I rode on the roads, rivers, seas, valleys and mountains in search of the truth behind our belief, the reason for pray and practices of spiritualties. This deeper perusal brought me before Lord Shiva. I was influenced by the complexity and wilderness of the Lord. I was also amazed by the benevolence and kindness that he parts with his worshippers. I engaged myself in studying the myths surrounding him through travelling to his exclusive abode known as Jyotirlinga. I was overwhelmed to see the enormous faith, belief and devotion people possess for the Lord. I realised the depth and extent the Lord Shiva is connected with us. Through a great degree we are dependent for satiating our spiritual appetite through Him.

Shiva is the God of all. He is worshipped by Devas (Gods), Asuras (Demons), humans, creatures, etc. The list goes on. People of different backgrounds and qualities worship Lord Shiva. They get blessed. Lord Shiva as the Supreme one blesses anyone who worships him in sincere devotion. He does not discriminate who the seeker is and what the past he has. Obviously He finds ways to protect dharma and never allow any evil to triumph over good. Shiva is the ultimate reality, the nature of Bliss itself and all complete in Himself. He is beyond description, beyond all manifestation, beyond limitation of form, time and space. He is eternal, infinite, all pervading, all knowing and all powerful.

"The Jyotirling – Human Faith Redefined" is my humble effort to talk about Lord Shiva. My effort does not construe as defying or an over indulgence. Let it be my feeble attempt to collate a few pebbles from the ocean of mystery associated with the Lord. To go into the mystery of the Jyotirling an understanding of the basic human traits was helpful. This necessitated reasonable research in the area of commonly unexplainable subjects with caution. These studies supported by my personal real time experience of pilgrimage forms the subject matter of the novel.

This work presents an illuminating approach in the perusal of spirituality and religion. It is purely a narrative presentation of author's way of describing Lord Shiva. It is in no way a presentation of thrusting any religious priorities. The Ritualistic worshipping of the Lord is willfully kept out of the scope of this write-up. They are left to our learned priests.

This Religiospiritual text is divided in two parts. Part I deals with the theoretical aspects of Mankind and its Creations. It explained Human attributes to upgrade on the prevailing knowledge about mysteries and traits of Lord Shiva. Part II narrates the travel story of actual pilgrimage experiencing the myths about the Jyotirlinga. Together they comprise my journey to the mythological world giving complete understanding of the Jyotirling Shrines and redefining my faith.

Om Namah Shivaya!!

Index

"I dedicate this book to my
beloved parents."

Part I

Mankind & Its Creations

[This part takes us through extol of the Absolute Supreme Being, the Brahman the Mysterious Saviour who saves the whole Universe whenever reason arises. It takes our passage step by step through the review of the human traits. These have embedded in them the ability to think rationally about the wellbeing of the fellow mankind. Some of relevant human attributes are discussed here to explain many of our social behaviours. In a simple manner complex attributes are explained for our understanding each other. Understanding human traits with respect to religion and spirituality brings in to light various myths about the Gods and the Power of Belief. The complexity of one of the Trinity Lord Shiva is tried to be explained. With a gradual treatment we are given to understand the myths associated with Lord Shiva, the Supreme Saviour through the mysterious Jyotirling.]

Chapter One

Insights into Human Traits

After the first life traced in the universe about 3.5 billion years ago, human being of the present form is said to have come into existence through a long and slow biological evolution between 200000 to 150000 years ago.

Humans were the only self aware, intelligent, creatures on earth. The need to survive as intelligent beings came with the need to explain the complexities of the universe both grand and infinitesimal. The creature that explored why the bush rustled in the wind lived longer than the creature, which ignored it. In most cases it was merely the wind. But in a few, it was a predator. The necessity to neutralize such a predator caused humans to explore possibilities. The need to explore the possibilities caused the need to find explanations. The need for explanations yielded conclusions, regardless of the preposterousness of those conclusions.

Over the millennia, human beings built a complex set of stories that explained natural phenomena. These also conveniently encompassed the very real necessity of passing on moral codes and cultural history. This necessity made Human beings to evolve as social animals. Human's very survival depended upon the ability to predict and model the complex behaviour of other people. The skills to absorb and predict the behaviour of others is hardwired into human being. It's therefore not surprising that primitive man coped with complex events by using those abilities. The climate, the ocean, the land, these capricious entities were easily represented as generous or vengeful persons unseen. By making these unknown forces into individuals with character it was easy for human mind to assimilate, perceive and understand them better. These facts are derived from the extracted tales of many religion— Hinduism, Buddhism, Judaism, Islam, Christianity, Shintoism, and Zoroastrianism. Three real factual reasons are common to all these. They are history of the universe according to "god", a manner of worshiping "god" (or "gods") and a moral code of conduct. What constitute the common thread in all these tales is that Human needed to pass on their history i.e. to communicate. This communication took the form, what becomes broadly termed as the religion. Religion thus evolved as the means of communication to future generation. It was genetically beneficial to our species to teach our descendants about our past and this perhaps came out voluntarily. True past is destined to teach the way forward. Distorted past would take us backward. This is a very real mammalian trait. Intertwined in these stories is the tale of how it all began, because we need to know, when our "history" doesn't even approach reality.

We blink to clear our vision. In the same way we pray to fulfil our wishes. Blinking is a physical process which we see. Praying is a mental process which one feels but other does not see. What we see is that person bows his head and closes his eyes. Why does he do this because he is guided by what is known as *Faith*, which leads him to *believe* in and the process he follows is known as *Spirituality*. The entire act he performs is said to be the part of what is known as *Religion*. Thus spirituality is said to form the expression of Religion.

From infancy, every human being possesses an innate sense that "there is something more than just me". They also possess a drive to discover what that might be. People seek the deeper meaning, purpose, and significance that exist in life, in relationships and in the things that happen to us. We recognize this basic striving as "Faith" from a naturalistic psychological perspective. It is a universal part of being human. Person focuses his or her faith (God, Temple, Nature, etc.) and the things he or she does to try to make a connection with those things (prayer, sacraments, hiking, and pilgrimage). This is the path a person's faith travels as it seeks meaning, purpose and significance to find out what that "something more" might be. This path is termed 'Spirituality'. Spirituality may thus refer to any kind of activity through which a person seeks meaning, especially a "search for the sacred." It may also refer to personal growth, blissful experience, or an encounter with one's own "inner dimension." A person tries to satisfy his or her faith by engaging in various spiritual practices and pursuits. He earns experience of articulating what is true and what is not. This articulation of experience by spiritual striving following one's faith is known as 'Belief'.

In pursue of the need to sustain and survive human beings moved from place to place. Thus their form of communication to their next generation also became different. This fact leads to believe the drive behind the different religion. Religion becomes the comprehensive means of communication among the community of people. This guides people who share similar beliefs. These people work together to provide support for going deeper into those beliefs. They also stand accountable for living up to those beliefs. Religion is the substance, the ground, and the depth of man's spiritual life. Religions codify beliefs into sacred texts. By means of rituals and moral practices Religion seek to facilitate the deepest possible connection with the beliefs the particular community holds.

In his book *"The Varieties of Religious Experience"*, the psychologist William James defined religion as "*the feelings, acts, and experiences of individual person in their solitude, so far as they apprehend themselves to stand in relation to whatever they may consider the divine*". By the term "divine" James meant "any object that is godlike, whether it be a concrete deity or not" to which the individual feels impelled to respond with solemnity and gravity.

The sociologist Durkheim in his seminal book *"The Elementary Forms of the Religious Life"* defined religion as a *"unified system of beliefs and practices relative to sacred things"*. By sacred things he meant things "set apart and forbidden—beliefs and practices uniting into single moral community called a Church or a Temple". Sacred things are not limited to gods or spirits. A sacred thing can be "a rock, a tree, a spring, a pebble, a piece of wood, a house, a script, a book- in a word, anything can be sacred". Religious beliefs, myths, dogmas and legends represent the nature of these sacred things and the virtues and powers which are attributed to them.

Chapter Two

Insights into Hinduism

Having learnt about general human traits next important thing is to proceed to specific aspects of religion. Before indulging into a discussion about High end of the God in terms of our faith, belief, spirituality and religion, we need to understand our own existence as follower of the Hinduism with absolute clarity.

Hinduism is a big ocean. I am really not sure whether anybody other than the *Supreme Being Itself* knows it in its entirety. The people who had dived in this ocean perhaps had acknowledged this fact. Hinduism is not a book of texts; it is a book of *Vedham* and S*idhdhi* that is knowledge and experience. These two are boundless and so is the Hinduism. One may spend the whole life in exploring the Hinduism but at the end may not have ever seen the other bank of it. An example will take us close to the understanding: Once a king wanted to know everything of the Supreme knowledge. So being a king spent all the days in reading the scriptures not concentrating in the government. One day while he was walking along the beach he saw a small boy taking a cup of water from the ocean and pouring it on the sand. The boy kept doing this continuously. The king could not stop wondering what the boy was trying to achieve. When he asked the boy, the reply forth came that he was trying to drain the ocean and went ahead with his routine. The king held him tight in his hands and asked, "You fool! You think you can dry the ocean with this small cup you have?" The boy patiently replied, "When our king tries to find out everything about the Supreme knowledge within his short span of life, why can't I dry this ocean with this small cup?"

Hinduism is an open-minded discipline. It is a discipline that does not use force on its follower. In other words it does not dictate the follower to act by one *step by step* recipe it gives, condemning all other recipes. In fact Hinduism is a discipline that allows many religions and philosophies like Shaivam, Vaishnavam and many others to coexist and grow.

The word Hinduism has its roots in the land around and beyond the river Indus on the other side of the Hindukush Mountain. It refers to the religion and philosophies that were prospering there originally. Later on it was spread throughout the world. But at some later periods of time its practice got limited only to the Indian subcontinent. The discipline has no founder for itself. Although in existence from the time undefined it does not declare itself as Hinduism. It was the people from outside who discovered the practice by the people of the land beyond the Hindukush Mountain. They called it by the name Hinduism. Thus the new discipline with nomenclature Hinduism came into existence. Originally the names that were used to refer to this discipline are *Vaidik Dharma* (meaning discipline of Vedas) and *Sanatan dharma* (meaning eternal discipline). It is important to note the fact that it is a discipline and not a religion by the terms as defined for most other religions.

Hinduism in reality is quite different from the normal religion definitions. It asks for a complete paradigm shift in terms of what is being looked for in a religion. While most of other religions have "well defined" boundaries, i.e. there would be one named God, one holy book, one founder, one set of rules, which the adherers must follow, Hinduism does not have these kind of definitions.

The most important and valuable aspect of the practice of this discipline is that it has not closed itself inside any contours. On the contrary it echoed the realistic representation of the limitlessness of knowledge and experience. It is absolutely open-minded. This is the religion that calls *"Let the good things come from all the directions of the world"* (Source: *Rig Veda*). Thus this practicing discipline nurtured the good concepts with a neutral mindset. So Hinduism is more a Dharma (Discipline) than a Religion. In general this is not the religion of just postulations. Very naturally this religion *does not force even the acceptance of God* to the followers. The Hindus are not threatened if they do not pray to God.

Hinduism does not invent God but it discovers. It neither stops at the human boundary confused and failing to go forward, but gets to the divine aspects supported by facts. This makes their findings more logical and realistic and even the super human descriptions experiencable if not explainable. These and many more features make this practicing discipline (religion) harmonious and meaningful for any time in present or future, for any land or creed. Hinduism is world's one of the oldest and third largest disciplines in terms of populations that follow it. It is worshiped by over one billion followers and is the majority religion in India, Nepal, Mauritius and Bali (Indonesia).

Hinduism is also called by some practitioners and scholars as Sanatana Dharma, "the eternal law". Scholars have noted that Hinduism is not about one view or opinion centered around one individual. It has no traditional ecclesiastical order, no centralized religious authorities, no governing body, no prophet(s) nor any binding holy book. Hindus can choose to be polytheistic (belief in many Gods), pantheistic (one that believes that a quality of the Divine is within all life or all things, but that there is no transcendent element of the Divine), monistic (the metaphysical view that all is of one essential essence, substance or energy) or atheistic (an absence of belief in the existence of deities).

Hinduism is universally appealing for the simple reason that it is based on the concept of origin on Universe and its link with human. Human here have preferred to imagine the stars, planets and satellites to be greatly associated with celestial powers. Hindu religion therefore have given a human face for each of these prowesses and tried to set a relationship with mankind. Dealing in Hinduism therefore means dealing with the Universe. Within this diffuse and open structure, spirituality in Hindu philosophy is an individual experience. It defines spiritual practice as one's journey towards moksha, awareness of self, the discovery of higher truths, true nature of reality, and a consciousness that is liberated and content.

Chapter Three

Insights into Hindu Philosophy

Every religion has its own philosophy. Hindu philosophy is linked by shared concepts, recognisable rituals, cosmology, shared textual resources, pilgrimage to sacred sites and the questioning of authority.

Hindu texts are classified into Shruti ("heard") and Smriti ("remembered"). These texts discuss theology, philosophy, mythology, Vedic yajna, Yoga and agamic rituals and temple building, among other topics. Major scriptures include the Vedas and the Upanishads, the Bhagavad Gita, and the Agamas (the theological treatises and practical manuals of divine worship, include the Tantras, Mantras and Yantras).

Traditionally, Hinduism identifies four *marga* (ways) of spiritual practice, namely Gyana yoga (the way of knowledge); Bhakti yoga (the way of devotion); and Karma yoga (the way of selfless action) and Raja yoga (the way of contemplation and meditation). Gyana marga is a path often assisted by a *guru* (teacher) in one's spiritual practice. Bhakti marga is a path of faith and devotion to deity or deities. The spiritual practice often includes chanting, singing and music (viz. *kirtans)* in front of idols, or images of one or more deity, or a devotional Holy symbol. Karma marga is the path of one's work. Here diligent practical work or *vartta* (profession) becomes in itself a spiritual practice. Work in daily life is perfected as a form of spiritual liberation and not for its material rewards. Raja marga is the path of cultivating necessary virtues, self-discipline, *tapas* (meditation), contemplation and self-reflection sometimes with isolation and renunciation of the world, to a pinnacle state called *Samadhi*. This state of *Samadhi* has been compared to peak experience.

Prominent themes in Hindu beliefs include among many, the four *Purusarthas*, the proper goals or aims of human life, namely Dharma (ethics/duties), Artha (prosperity/work), Kama (emotions/sexuality) and Moksha (liberation/freedom); *Karma* (action, intent and consequences), *samsara* (cycle of rebirth) and the various Yogas (paths or practices to attain moksha). Hindu practices include rituals such as puja (worship) and recitations, meditation, family-oriented rites of passage, annual festivals, and occasional pilgrimages. Some Hindus leave their social world and material possessions, then engage in lifelong Sannyasa (ascetic practices) to achieve moksha. Hinduism prescribes the eternal duties, such as honesty, refraining from injuring living beings (ahimsa), patience, forbearance, self-restraint, and compassion, among others.

Hindu philosophy adores worship as an act of religious devotion usually directed to one or more Hindu deities. When we worship our God, it comes from a different place within our spirit. It is the art of losing self in the adoration of God being greater. A sense of Bhakti or devotional love is generally invoked. This term is probably a central one in Hinduism. Hindus usually perform worship to achieve some specific end or to integrate the body, the mind and the spirit in order to help the performer evolve into a higher being Deities. We cannot worship until we enter His courts with praises. Within Hinduism a large number of personal gods (Ishvaras) are worshipped as murtis. These beings are either aspects of the supreme Brahman, Avatars of the Supreme Being, or significantly powerful entities known as Devas. The exact nature of belief in regards to each deity varies between differing Hindu denominations and philosophies. Often these beings are depicted in humanoid or partially humanoid forms, complete with a set of unique and complex iconography in each case. These deities may be different but they are generally all considered forms of the one God (Brahman). These deities and their Pujas (religious rituals) provide one of the ways to communicate with this one divinity.

Contrary to prevailing misconceptions, Hindus all worship one Supreme Being, though by different names. This is because the people of India with different languages and cultures have understood the one God in their own distinct way. Through history there arose four principal Hindu denominations—Saivism, Shaktism, Vaishnavism and Smartaism. For Saivites, God is Siva. For Shaktas, Goddess Shakti is supreme. For Vaishnavites, Lord Vishnu is God. For Smartas—who see all Deities as reflections of the One God—the choice of Deity is left to the devotee. This liberal Smarta perspective is well known, but it is not the prevailing Hindu view. Due to this diversity, Hindus are profoundly tolerant of other religions, respecting the fact that each has its own pathway to the one God. One of the unique understandings in Hinduism is that God is not far away, living in a remote heaven, but is inside each and every soul, in the heart and consciousness, waiting to be discovered. This knowing that God is always with us gives us hope and courage. Knowing the One Great God in this intimate and experiential way is the goal of Hindu spirituality.

Hinduism is both monotheistic and henotheistic. Monotheism has been defined as the belief in the existence of only one god that created the world. It is all-powerful and intervenes in the world. It reflects in the traditions of the Bahai Faith, Balinese Hinduism, Christianity, Hindu sects such as Shaivism and Vaishnavism, Islam, Judaism, Sikhism, and Zoroastrianism. Henotheism (from Greek meaning "one god") is the worship of a single god while not denying the existence or possible existence of other deities. It is a religious system in which the believer worships one god without denying that others may worship different gods with equal validity.

Polytheistic believes that there are many equal Gods. Hindus were never polytheistic. Henotheism better defines the Hindu view. It means the worship of one God without denying the existence of other Gods. We Hindus believe in the one all-pervasive God who energizes the entire universe. We can see Him in the life shining out of the eyes of humans and all creatures. This view of God as existing in and giving life to all things is called panentheism. It is different from pantheism, which is the belief that God is the natural universe and nothing more. It is also different from strict theism which says God is only above the world, apart and transcendent. Panentheism is an all-encompassing concept. It says that God is both in the world and beyond it, both immanent and transcendent. That is the highest Hindu view.

Hindus also believe in many gods based on various functions they perform. Not getting confused with the Supreme Being, these divinities are highly advanced beings that have specific duties and powers. Each denomination worships the Supreme God and its own pantheon of divine beings. What is sometimes confusing to non-Hindus is that Hindus of various sects may call the one God by many different names, according to their denomination or regional tradition. Truth for the Hindu has many names, but that does not make for many truths. Hinduism gives us the freedom to approach God in our own way. It encourages a multiplicity of paths, not asking for conformity to just one. Some Hindus believe only in the formless Absolute Reality as God. Others believe in God as personal Lord and Creator. This freedom makes the understanding of God in Hinduism, the oldest living religion, the richest in all of Earth's existing faiths.

Chapter Four

Insights into Elements of Hinduism

Hindus believe the soul is immortal and takes birth time and time again. Hindus believe in reincarnation. Carnate means "of flesh," and reincarnate means to "re-enter the flesh." Life and death are realities for all of us. Hinduism believes that the soul never dies, but inhabits one body after another on the Earth during its evolutionary journey. Like the caterpillar's transformation into a butterfly, physical death is a most natural transition for the soul, which survives and guided by karma, continues its long pilgrimage until it is one with God. Our ancient scriptures the Vedas reveal the reality of Reincarnation. At death the soul leaves the physical body. But the soul does not die. It lives on in a subtle body called the astral body. The astral body exists in the nonphysical dimension called the astral plane. It is also the world we are in during our dreams at night when we sleep. Such experiences continue until we are reborn again in another physical body as a baby.

Each reincarnating soul chooses a home and a family conducive to fulfill its next step of learning and maturation. After many lifetimes of following dharma, the soul is fully matured in love, wisdom and knowledge of God. There is no longer a need for physical birth, for all lessons have been learned, all karmas fulfilled. That soul is then liberated, freed from the cycle of birth, death and rebirth. Evolution then continues in the more refined spiritual worlds. This can be explained by a simple fact that after we graduate from elementary school we never have to go back to the fifth grade. We have gone beyond that level in understanding. Thus, life's ultimate goal is not in following any natural pursuits (money, clothes, sex, power, food or any other of the instinctive needs). The ultimate goal is the rare and priceless objects of life - enlightenment and liberation. This Hindu view of the soul's evolution answers many otherwise bewildering questions. It removes the fear of death by giving assurance that each soul is evolving toward the same spiritual destiny.

Hindus believe that Karma and reincarnation are leading every single soul to God Realization. Karma is the universal principle of cause and effect. When something happens to us that are apparently unfortunate or unjust, it is not God punishing us. It is the result of our own past actions. Our actions, both good and bad, come back to us in the future, helping us to learn from life's lessons and we become better people. The Vedas tell us if we sow goodness, we will reap goodness; if we sow evil, we will reap evil. Thus we create our own destiny through thought and action. Karma is one of the natural laws of the mind, just as gravity is a law of matter. Just as the God created gravity to bring order to the physical world, He created karma as a divine system of justice that is self-governing and infinitely fair. It automatically creates the appropriate future experience in response to the current action. Understanding the way karma works, we seek to live a good and virtuous life through right thought, right speech and right action. This is called Dharma.

Karma is basically energy. I throw energy out through thoughts, words and deeds and it comes back to me in time through other people. Karma is our best teacher which teaches us that we must always face the consequences of our actions and thus improve and refine our behavior or suffer if we do not. We Hindus look at time as a circle, as things cycle around again. Professor Einstein came to the same conclusion. He saw time as a curve and space as well. This would eventually make a circle. Karma is a very just law which like gravity treats everyone the same. Because Hindus understand karma, they do not hate or resent people who do harm to them. Hindus take it as if the people are giving back the effects of the causes that they we set in motion at an earlier time. The law of karma puts man at the center of responsibility for everything he does and everything that is done to him.

The process of action and reaction on all levels—physical, mental and spiritual—is karma. For example, I say kind words to you, and you feel peaceful and happy. I say harsh words to you, and you become ruffled and upset. The kindness and the harshness will return to me, through others, at a later time. This is karma. An architect thinks creative, productive thoughts while drawing plans for a new building. But would he to think destructive, unproductive thoughts would soon not allow him to accomplish any kind of positive task even if he desired to do so. This is karma, a natural law of the mind. We must also be very careful about our thoughts, because thought creates, and thoughts make karmas—good, bad and mixed. This also forms a very complex subject of Hinduism.

Hindus worship God through the image. We invoke the presence of God from the higher, unseen worlds, into the image so that we can commune with Him and receive His blessings. The stone or metal deity images in Hindu temples are not mere symbols of the Gods. They are the form through which their love, power and blessings flood forth into this world. This can be clear from the following example. In our telephonic conversation we do not talk to the telephone, rather we use telephone as a means of communication with another person. Without the telephone we could not have conversed across long distances. Likewise without the sanctified icon in the temple we cannot easily commune with the Deity. Divinity can be invoked and felt in a stone, in sacred fire, or in a tree, or in the enlightened person of a Guru. In our temples God is invoked in the sanctum by highly trained priests. Through the practice of yoga, or meditation, we invoke God inside ourselves. Yoga means to attach oneself to God within. The image or icon of worship is a focus for our prayers and devotions. Another way to explain icon worship is to acknowledge that Hindus believe God is everywhere, in all things, whether stone, wood, creatures or people. So it is not surprising that they feel comfortable worshiping the Divine in His material manifestation. The Hindu can see God in stone and water, fire, air and ether, and inside his own soul.

In Hinduism one of the ultimate attainments is when the seeker goes beyond the need of all form and symbol. This is the yogi's goal. In this way Hinduism is the least idol-oriented of all the religions of the world. There is no religion that is more aware of the transcendent, timeless, formless, causeless Truth. Nor is there any religion which uses more symbols to represent Truth in preparation for that realization. All religions have their symbols of Holiness through which the sacredness flows into the mundane. To name a few - the Christian cross, or statues of Mother Mary and Saint Theresa, the Holy Kaaba in Mecca, the Sikh Adi Granth enshrined in the Golden Temple in Amritsar, the Arc and Torah of the Jews, the image of a meditating Buddha, the totems of indigenous and Pagan faiths. Such icons, or graven images, are held in awe by the idol worshipers' of the respective great faiths. The human mind releases itself from suffering through the use of forms and symbols that awaken reverence evoke sanctity and spiritual wisdom. Even a fundamentalist Christian, who rejects all forms of idol worship, including those of the Catholic and Episcopal churches, would resent someone who showed disrespect for his Bible. This is because he considers it sacred. His book and the Hindu's icon are much alike in this way.

Chapter Five

The Veda & Spread of Hinduism

The Veda is the Sacred Holy book of the Hindus. The Veda, which means "wisdom," is comprised of four ancient and Holy Scriptures. Hindus revere these as the revealed word of God. Like the Taoist Tao te Ching, the Buddhist Dhammapada, the Sikh Adi Granth, the Jewish Torah, the Christian Bible and the Muslim Koran—the Veda is the Hindu holy book.

There are four books of the Vedas —Rig, Yajur, Sama and Atharva which include over 100,000 verses. The knowledge imparted by the Vedas ranges from earthy devotion to high philosophy. Their words and wisdom permeate Hindu thought, ritual and meditation. The ultimate scriptural authority for Hindus, the Vedas originated as early as 6000 BCE. Initially it was transmitted through oral utterances and later was written down in Sanskrit. The Veda constitutes the world's longest and most ancient scripture. It open a rare window into untold centuries unto today, ancient Indian society, proclaiming life's sacredness and the way to oneness with God. All Hindus wholeheartedly accept the Vedas, yet each draws selectively, interprets freely and amplifies abundantly. Over time, this multiple thread of tolerant allegiance has woven the varied multi-coloured tapestry of Indian Hindu Dharma and enabled its spread. Each of the four Vedas has four sections: Samhita (hymn collections), Brahmanas (priestly manuals), Aranyakas (forest treatises) and Upanishads (enlightened discourses). The Samhita and Brahmanas affirm that God is imminent and transcendent and prescribe ritual worship, mantra and devotional hymns to establish communication with the spiritual worlds. The hymns are invocations to the One Divine and to the Divinities of nature, such as the Sun, the Rain, the Wind, the Fire and the Dawn — as well as prayers for matrimony, progeny, prosperity, concord, protection, domestic rites and more. The Aranyakas and Upanishads outline the soul's evolutionary journey, provide yogic philosophical training and propound realization of man's oneness with God as the destiny of all souls. The Vedas advice: "Let there be no neglect of Truth. Let there be no neglect of dharma. Let there be no neglect of welfare. Let there be no neglect of prosperity. Let there be no neglect of study and teaching. Let there be no neglect of the duties to the Gods and the ancestors" (Taittiriya Upanishad 1.11.1). "United your resolve, united your hearts, may your spirits be one that you may long together dwell in unity and concord!" (RigVeda10.191.4). "There, where there is no darkness, nor night, nor day, nor being, nor nonbeing, there is the Auspicious One, alone, absolute and eternal. There is the glorious splendor of that Light from whom in the beginning sprang ancient wisdom" (Shvetashvatara Upanishad 4.18). "Taking as a bow the great weapon of the Upanishad, one should put upon it an arrow sharpened by meditation. Stretching it with a thought directed to the essence of that, penetrate that Imperishable as the mark, my friend" (Mundaka Upanishad 2.2.3).

In Hindu disciple our God is often depicted with a spouse in our traditional stories. However, on a deeper philosophical level, God and God's energy are one, and the metaphor of the inseparable divine couple serves only to illustrate this Oneness. The Supreme Being and the Gods are neither male nor female and are therefore not married. Those who learn the higher Hindu philosophies know that Gods are neither male nor female. In fact, attaining to that Godly level of being is one of the mystical goals of yoga. This is accomplished in Yoga by blending the feminine and masculine currents, Ida and pingala, into the spiritual current, sushumna, in the center of the spine within each individual.

Hindus honour all religious traditions and the people within them. We regard our faith as uniquely endowed. We also believe that there is no exclusive path, no one way for all. In India, where Hindus are the overwhelming majority, the rights of minority religions have always been honored. Hindus have welcomed, embraced and lived peacefully along with other religions for centuries. During those periods Hinduism itself evolved into hundreds of strains. These made Hindus to be fully at home with many different traditions and viewpoints within their own faith. Hence Hindus are naturally tolerant of other religions. They respect each of their unique beliefs, practices, goals and paths of attainment. They do not object when the doctrines of one conflict with those of another. Hinduism never teaches disrespecting other religion or disgracing followers of it. This beautiful mind of the Hindu attitude has been well summarized in the following Sanskrit Verse:

"As the different streams, having their sources in different places, mingle their water in the sea, so, O Lord, the different paths which men take through different tendencies, various though they appear, crooked or straight, all lead to Thee."

When discussing other religions, Hindu leaders often quote a verse from the *Rig Veda*: Sat, *viprah bahudha vadanti,"* meaning "Truth is One, sages describe it variously." It conveys a core Hindu idea: that there can be multiple valid viewpoints about the Supreme. Dr. S. Radhakrishnan, philosopher and former president of India, stressed this point: *"The Hindu recognizes one Supreme Spirit, though different names are given to it."* It simply says that all religions revere the One Truth; all believe in the One Supreme

Being. Their beliefs and practices are different; their paths are distinct.

Hindus share values common to all faiths. They are piety, love of God, respect for tradition, a stress on duty, responsibility and basic human virtues, such as nonviolence, truthfulness, compassion and charity. The heart of a religion is its understanding of the soul's relationship to God. Hinduism and most Eastern religions believe that, at the highest level, God and soul are one, inseparable, while Western faiths maintain that Creator and creation are eternally distinct.

I said at the beginning of the Chapter 2 that Hinduism is a big ocean. I am really not sure whether anybody other than the Supreme Being Itself knows it in its entirety. Hinduism is an open-minded discipline. This is the religion that calls ***"Let the good things come from all the directions of the world"*** **(Source: *Rig Veda*)**. Thus this religion nurtured the good concepts with a neutral mindset. Hinduism is a Dharma (Discipline) than a Religion. Hinduism prospers and sustain through natural propagation through its open door which remains accessible to all on all occasions. The fragrance of Hinduism propagates on its merit. People of any origin take its pleasure and dip into its ocean forever. To do so one does not need any broker as Hinduism does not believe in broking. It is difficult to comprehend this great exhaustive oldest discipline of the world in a small chapter like this. It is difficult as well to comprehend to end the discussion on this openly loved and sweetly endorsed practicing discipline.

Chapter Six

About Lord Shiva

We are much enlightened by now in the lights enshrined in Hinduism. More inquisitiveness further leads us to know about Lord Shiva. Shiva is the Lord of the Lords. It is not easy to write and explain everything about Lord Shiva. Many have tried to explain him and praised him as per their knowledge. But the explanation is endless. It is unthinkable from a human being when even Devas, Asuras and other Sages and Rishimunis have very little words to explain about the Lord almighty. Therefore before going ahead to understand Lord Shiva let us clear our basic pillar of perception of Hinduism.

The Trimurti is a concept in Hinduism in which the entire Universal Cycle of cosmic functions have been imagined or considered to be consisting of three stages. Hindu religion has associated a human personification with each stage. First stage of the cosmic function of the Universal cycle is considered to be Creation. Hindu Religion has associated the personified form of Lord Brahma, the Creator with it. Once Universe is created including the life in it, Cycle yields to the next stage of the cosmic function where the creation has to be sustained, grown, propagated and preserved. With this stage Hindu Religion has associated the personified form of Lord Vishnu as the Preserver. The third or the last stage of the cosmic function of the Universal Cycle is considered and assumed to be the most difficult stage. Hindu Religion has assumed in one side that there existed threats for destruction of the Universe and the humanity, while on the other side the Universe containing the life cannot be destroyed. Thus it makes the third stage of the cosmic function as the most difficult of the three. Hindu Religion has associated the personified form of Lord Shiva as the Handler of this toughest task. Thus Lord Shiva represents the aspect of the Supreme Being (Brahman of the Upanishads) that continuously dissolves to recreate in the cyclic process of creation, preservation, dissolution and recreation of the universe.

Owing to His cosmic activity of dissolution and recreation, the words destroyer and destruction have been erroneously associated with Lord Shiva. This difficulty arises when people fail to grasp the true significance of His cosmic role. The creation sustains itself by a delicate balance between the opposing forces of good and evil. When the balance is disturbed and sustenance of life becomes impossible, Lord Shiva dissolves the universe for creation of the next cycle. It is then that the unliberated souls will have another opportunity to liberate themselves from bondage with the physical world. Thus, Lord Shiva protects the souls from pain and suffering that would be caused by a dysfunctional universe. This important eternal fact is best understood by comparing analogous cyclic processes that winter is essential for spring to appear and the night is necessary for the morning to follow. To further illustrate, a goldsmith does not destroy gold when he melts old irreparable golden jewelry to create beautiful new ornaments.

Lord Shiva is the Lord of mercy and compassion. He protects devotees from evil forces such as lust, greed, and anger. He grants boons, bestows grace and awakens wisdom in His devotees.

In Sanskrit the word "Siva" means "The Auspicious One". Lord Shiva is the chief deity within Shaivism. Shaivism is one of the oldest of the four major sects of Hinduism. Followers of Shaivism, called "Shaivas" revere Shiva as the Supreme Being. The *Shiva Purana* is one of the Puranas (Puranas are a genre of

Hindu religious texts) dedicated to Shiva. Shaivism is widespread mostly throughout India, Nepal, and Sri Lanka. Other areas notable for the practice of Shaivism include parts of Southeast Asia, especially Malaysia, Singapore, and Indonesia. His 'Transformer' form is one of the five primary forms of God in the Smarta Tradition.

At the highest level, Shiva is regarded as limitless, transcendent, unchanging and formless. Shiva also has many benevolent and fearsome forms. In benevolent aspects, he is depicted as an omniscient Yogi who lives an ascetic life on Mount Kailash, as well as a householder with wife Parvati and his two children, Ganesha and Kartikeya. In fierce aspects, he is often depicted slaying demons.

Chapter Seven

Mystery of Origin of Shiva

In the Vedic literature the Rigveda a minor atmospheric deity with fearsome powers is mentioned as Rudra. In the same text there is also a mention of Shiva. But its mention is simply as an epithet that means "kind, auspicious", one of the adjectives used to describe many different Vedic deities. Scholars have identified Rudra with fierce ruthless natural phenomenon and storm, while the beneficial rains that follow are welcomed as Shiva aspect of him. This healing, nurturing, life-enabling aspect emerges in the Vedas as Rudra-Shiva and in the post-Vedic literature ultimately as Shiva. Shiva combines the destructive and constructive powers, the terrific and the gentle, as the ultimate recycler and rejuvenator of all existence.

Incidentally scholars have noticed above contrasting aspects of Shiva in the Greek god Dionysus. Besides Shiva's iconic associations with bull, snakes, anger, bravery, dancing and carefree life also found to be similar with the Greek god. In fact Alexander, the Great conqueror had mentioned Shiva as "Indian Dionysus". Some scholars also noticed the use of phallic symbol as an icon for Shiva was similar to that for Irish, Nordic, Greek (Dionysus) and Roman deities. There was similarity with the idea of this aniconic column linking heaven and earth prevalent among early Indo-Aryans. There are other opinions contested which suggest Shiva to have emerged from indigenous pre-Aryan tribal origins.

The birth of the three Gods comprising Hindu Holy trinity is a great mystery in itself. While many puranas believe that God Brahma and God Vishnu were born from God Shiva, there is no hardcore evidence to prove the same. This brings forward the mystery about Shiva's origin. Many Hindus believe that God Shiva is a Swyambhu – which means He is not born from a human body. He was created automatically. He was there when there was nothing and He will remain even after everything is destructed. That is why he is also lovingly called as the 'Adi-Dev' which means the 'Oldest God in the Hindu mythology'.

There go many stories suggesting the creation of this mighty Lord. Shiva Purana narrated a very interesting story. One day, Lord Brahma and Lord Vishnu were both arguing about their powers. Both of them wanted to prove that one is mightier than the other. Right then, amidst the heated discussion, an inexplicable blazing pillar of light appeared in front of them, whose root and tip were not visible. The roots seemed to penetrate deep into the earth with the tip piercing into the skies beyond eternity. Both the Gods were amazed by the view of this pillar. They wondered about this third entity that stood there challenging both of their supremacy. Soon their argument subdued. They started thinking how to deal with this new entity. Suddenly, they heard an oracle out of nowhere, which asked them to compete with one another. They both had to find the start and end of the blazing pillar.

Both Brahma and Vishnu set out to locate the start and end of that pillar. Brahma turned himself into a goose and flew upwards to find the top of the pillar. Vishnu transformed himself into a boar and dug deep into the earth to find the end of the pillar. Both tried tirelessly. The search went on for ages but the outcome proved futile as neither of them succeeded in their respective missions.

After their unsuccessful attempts, both Lord Brahma and Lord Vishnu felt humbled. They came back to their original place only to find Lord Shiva manifesting in front of them. That made them realize that there was already another ultimate power ruling this universe and that was God Shiva. They understood that Shiva's power and cosmic existence is much beyond their imagination. They in fact realised, it was Lord Shiva who was more powerful than both of them. The eternity of the pillar actually symbolizes the never-ending eternity of God Shiva. The fiery column of energy was the form of appearance of Lord Shiva. Since then worshipping of Shiva took the form of Linga. Linga Purana's energy form of Shiva merges with the fiery form of Rudra of the Shiva Purana.

Lord Shiva is therefore no ordinary god. He is very mystifying. His ways can never be interpreted by the earthly norms and definitions. He performs multiple roles and wields a mighty power over the universe. He takes delight in occupying crematory grounds. His favourite dress code is animal skin with skull garlands. He is always accompanied by a large battalion of fierce-looking demons. They are also bloodthirsty. They can devastate anything with a sweeping operation. The entire troop of Lord Shiva and his army are considered strange. They are believed to constantly engage in carrying out the multifaceted mission of the Lord in all the known worlds and beyond.

While Lord Shiva is mostly known as a ferocious god, he has another mysterious side too. He is known to spend long periods of time in deep meditation in the lofty Himalayas. This absolute silence and stillness on one hand and the vibrant and ferocious exploits on the other hand, makes it very hard to understand Lord's original nature.

Theologically saying there is a border between spiritual planets and material world. It divides material world from Spiritual world. In the form of Swyambhu, Shiva always exists in the spiritual world. Brahma Samhita suggests that there is no separate birth. Therefore to help in Lord's material creation he will born as Rudra. Those who are Sattvic in nature they will worship Lord Shiva in Swyambhu form. Other like Aghora who are in tamasic, rajasic will worship in Rudra form.

About Lord Shiva's origin our Upanishads and Puranas postulated varied kind of ideas, which did not satisfy Vyas deva. So Narada came to him. He guided him to write a Purana which is of sattvic nature. By this write up people of Kali Yuga would understand more clearly about the reality of God. So Vyas deva wrote Srimad Bhagavatam (known as Bhagwata Purana). This is considered as the ultimate Purana. After writing that Vyasa was satisfied and believed that one would help the people of Kali Yuga. As per this Purana Lord Shiva's birth is associated with the following event:

When Brahma decided to commence the sequence of creation, he first of all created four Kumars by just having a wish in his mind. They were Sanaka, Sanandana, Sanatana and Sanatkumara. These four Kumars were all embodiments of pure qualities. They did not possess any negative qualities. Brahma had created them to take forward the process of creation. But they refused when they were ordered by Brahma to do so. They said, "No, we are not going to be entangled in these material affairs. We shall remain bachelors and preach the glories of Godhead". Hearing this Brahma became angry. And while he was angry, from his anger Rudra was produced from his forehead.

The Endless Column of fire witnessed by Lord Brahma and Lord Vishnu had convinced both about the prior existence of the greatest power (Adi Deva). Thus in short Shiva is the indestructible and boundless Energy. Shiva is not born. He always existed, exists and will exist for ever. That's why he is called Bhava; means 'is there' always at any time. He is the only God, who has been praised as neither born, nor dead. There is Narayanodbhavam, meaning something existed before he came. There is no Shivodbhavam. Vedas have mentioned very clearly that, "kevalaha Rudraha, na dwitheeyam" meaning, only Rudra, nothing else. The essence of Vedas is that there are three states of Godliness. Firstly Shiva as Nirguna Nirakar as Paramjyothi state; Secondly as Shiva Linga, the Aroopa state, where neither Nirakar nor Sakar, but as an unborn child state representative of the early universe (Hiranya Garbha) and the third state is Sakar Narayana, who represents as the Lord of the universe. When Brahma sought help in creation of humans and other races, including Devas, Yaksharas, Kinnaras, Nagas etc, Shiva and Shakti appeared as Uma Maheshwara and hence they are called as father and mother.

Chapter Eight

Attributes of Lord Shiva

The handler of the most complicated part of the Cosmic Cycle has been visualised by the Hindus in the form of Lord Shiva. Since this cosmic operation involves destruction of the evil, simultaneous regeneration or creation is to be ensured by him. These two functions necessarily involve energy to be spent in varied directions. Carrying out the numerous tasks Lord Shiva is imagined to be equipped with multitasked source of energy. Thus it is difficult to symbolise Him in one particular Form. Hindus have symbolised Lord Shiva with multiple attributes for carrying out various functions. The symbolism discussed below includes major symbols that are common to all pictures and images of Shiva venerated by Hindus. For this reason the images of Shiva vary significantly in their symbolism.

The unclad body covered with ashes: The unclad body symbolizes the transcendental aspect of the Lord. Since most things reduce to ashes when burned, ashes symbolize the physical universe. The ashes on the unclad body of the Lord signify that Shiva is the source of the entire universe which emanates from Him, but He transcends the physical phenomena and is not affected by it.

Matted locks: Lord Shiva is the Master of yoga. The three matted locks on the head of the Lord convey the idea that integration of the physical, mental and spiritual energies is the ideal of yoga.

Ganga: Ganga (river Ganges) is associated with Hindu mythology as the most sacred river of the Hindus. According to Legend, one who bathes in Ganga in accordance with traditional rites and ceremonies on religious occasions in combination with certain astrological events is believed to be freed from sin. He attains knowledge, purity and peace. Ganga is symbolically represented on the head of the Lord by a female (Mother Ganga) with a jet of water emanating from her mouth and falling on the ground. This signifies that the Lord destroys sin, removes ignorance, and bestows knowledge, purity and peace on the devotees.

The crescent moon: It is shown on one side of the Lord's head as an ornament, and not as an integral part of His countenance. The waxing and waning phenomenon of the moon symbolizes the time cycle through which creation evolves from the beginning to the end. Since the Lord is the Eternal Reality, He is beyond time. Thus, the crescent moon is only one of His ornaments, and not an integral part of Him.

Three eyes: Lord Shiva, also called Tryambaka Deva (literally, "three-eyed Lord"), is depicted as having three eyes. The Sun is His right eye, the Moon the left eye and fire the third eye. The two eyes on the right and left indicate His activity in the physical world. The third eye in the center of the forehead symbolizes spiritual knowledge and power, and is thus called the eye of wisdom or knowledge. Like fire, the powerful gaze of Shiva's third eye annihilates evil, and thus the evil-doers fear His third eye.

Half-open eyes: when the Lord opens His eyes, a new cycle of creation emerges and when He closes them, the universe dissolves for creation of the next cycle. The half-open eyes convey the idea that creation is going through cyclic process, with no beginning and no end. Lord Shiva is the Master of Yoga, as He uses His yogic power to project the universe from Himself. The half-open eyes also symbolize His yogic posture.

Kundalas (two ear rings): Two Kundalas, Alakshya (meaning "which cannot be shown by any sign") and Niranjan (meaning "which cannot be seen by mortal eyes") in the ears of the Lord signify that He is beyond ordinary perception. Since the kundala in the left ear of the Lord is of the type used by women and the one in His right ear is of the type used by men, these Kundalas also symbolize the Shiva and Shakti (male and female) principle of creation.

Snake around the neck: Sages have used snakes to symbolize the yogic power of Lord Shiva with which He dissolves and recreates the universe. Like a yogi, a snake hoards nothing, carries nothing, builds nothing, lives on air alone for a long time, and lives in mountains and forests. The venom of a snake, therefore, symbolizes the yogic power.

A snake (Vasuki Naga): It is shown curled three times around the neck of the Lord and is looking towards His right side. The three coils of the snake symbolize the past, present and future - time in cycles. The Lord wearing the curled snake like an ornament signifies that creation proceeds in cycles and is time dependent, but the Lord Himself transcends time. The right side of the body symbolizes the human activities based upon knowledge, reason and logic. The snake looking towards the right side of the Lord signifies that the Lord's eternal laws of reason and justice preserve natural order in the universe.

Rudraksha necklace: Rudra is another name of Shiva. Rudra also means "strict or uncompromising" and aksha means "eye." Rudraksha necklace worn by the Lord illustrates that He uses His cosmic laws firmly - without compromise - to maintain law and order in the universe. The necklace has 108 beads each of which symbolise the elements that were used in the creation of the world.

Varda Mudra: the Lord's right hand is shown in a boon-bestowing and blessing pose. As stated earlier, Lord Shiva annihilates evil, grants boons, bestows grace, destroys ignorance, and awakens wisdom in His devotees.

Trident (Trishula): A three-pronged trident shown adjacent to the Lord symbolises His three fundamental powers (Shakti) of will (iccha), action (kriya) and knowledge (jnana). The trident also symbolises Lord's power to destroy evil and ignorance.

Damaru (Drum): A small drum with two sides separated from each other by a thin neck-like structure symbolizes the two utterly dissimilar states of existence, unmanifest and manifest. When a damaru is vibrated, it produces dissimilar sounds which are fused together by resonance to create one sound. The sound thus produced symbolises Nada, the cosmic sound of AUM, which can be heard during deep meditation. According to Hindu scriptures, Nada is the source of creation.

Kamandalu: A water pot (Kamandalu) made from a dry pumpkin contains nectar and is shown on the ground next to Shiva. The process of making Kamandalu has deep spiritual significance. A ripe pumpkin is plucked from a plant, its fruit is removed and the shell is cleaned for containing the nectar. In the same way, an individual must break away from attachment to the physical world and clean his inner self of egoistic desires in order to experience the bliss of the Self, symbolised by the nectar in the Kamandalu.

Nandi: The bull is associated with Shiva and is said to be His vehicle. The bull symbolises both power and ignorance. Lord Shiva's use of the bull as a vehicle conveys the idea that He removes ignorance and bestows power of wisdom on His devotees. The bull is called Vrisha in Sanskrit. Vrisha also means dharma (righteousness). Thus a bull shown next to Shiva also indicates that He is the etemal companion of righteousness.

Tiger skin: A tiger skin symbolizes potential energy. Lord Shiva, sitting on or wearing a tiger skin, illustrates the idea that He is the source of the creative energy that remains in potential form during the dissolution state of the universe. Of His own Divine Will the Lord activates the potential form of the creative energy to project the universe in endless cycles.

Cremation ground: Shiva sitting in the cremation ground signifies that He is the controller of death in the physical world. Since birth and death are cyclic, controlling one implies controlling the other. Thus, Lord Shiva is revered as the ultimate controller of birth and death in the phenomenal world.

Lord Shiva is 'shakti' or power; Shiva is the destroyer, the most powerful god of the Hindu pantheon and one of the godheads in the Hindu Trinity. Known by many names - Mahadeva, Mahayogi, Pashupati, Nataraja, Bhairava, Vishwanath, Bhava, Bhole Nath - Lord Shiva is perhaps the most complex of Hindu deities. Hindus recognize this Ombudsmen feature of Lord Shiva by putting his shrine in the temple separate from those of the other deities worshiped by the Hindus.

Hindus belief Lord Shiva is absolute. He does not have any parents. He never takes birth and is all alone without association with any of the creatures or creations enjoying in the Self. To Hindus Lord Shiva is the only one to whom anybody can surrender as it is the only perennial Being. Hence God is the Lord of all creatures (lives/souls). Going forward the Lord is hailed as Pashupati (Lord of living beings). Whether it is devas or asuras or humans or other creatures all are Pashus. That being the case the

Lord cannot be partial to any one section of Pashus. So anybody who worships the Lord Shiva sincerely could get blessed with his Grace irrespective of the caste, creed, race, power, status and qualities.

Lord Shiva is the God of all. Like the mother He showers the grace for all the children, but the abusing children get punished. This Supreme Lord is even better than a mother as he does not withhold the grace. He is our beloved Pashupati. The God would not be biased. It would not differentiate between groups, whether it be divines or demons or humans or plats or creatures or on sex or on race etc. All that matters to him is dharma and the pure devotion towards it. No doubt this lovely Lord Shiva is worshipped alike by divines, demons, scholars, less educated poor simple human and the other creatures.

Chapter Nine

The Cult of Shiva

Shaivism is the branch in the Hinduism that discuss exclusively about Lord Shiva. It is one of the four major sects of Hinduism, the others being Vaishnavism, Shaktism and the Smarta Tradition. Followers of Shaivism are called "Shaivas". They revere Shiva as the Supreme Being. Shaivas believe that Shiva is All and in all the creator, preserver, destroyer, revealer and concealer of all that is. He is not only the creator in Shaivism, he is the creation that results from him and he is everything and everywhere. Shiva is considered the primal soul, the pure consciousness and Absolute Reality in the Shaiva traditions.

The Shaivism theology is broadly grouped into two: the popular theology influenced by Shiva-Rudra in the Vedas, Epics and the Puranas; and the esoteric theology influenced by the Shiva and Shakti-related Tantra texts. The Vedic-Brahmanic Shiva theology includes both monist (advaita) and devotional traditions (dvaita) such as Tamil Shaiva Siddhanta and Lingayatism with temples featuring items such as linga, Shiva-Parvati iconography, bull Nandi within the premises, relief artwork showing mythologies and aspects of Shiva.

The Tantric Shiva tradition ignored the mythologies and Puranas related to Shiva. It developed a spectrum of practices depending on the sub-school. For example, historical records suggest the tantric Kapalikas (literally, the "skull-men") co-existed with and shared many Vajrayana Buddhist rituals. They were engaged in esoteric practices that revered Shiva and Shakti wearing skulls, begged with empty skulls, used meat, alcohol as a part of ritual. In contrast, the esoteric tradition within Kashmir

Shaivism has featured the Karma and Trika sub-traditions. The Karma sub-tradition focused on esoteric rituals around Shiva-Kali pair. The Trika sub-tradition developed a theology of triads involving Shiva, combined it with an ascetic lifestyle focusing on personal Shiva in the pursuit of monistic self liberation.

According to another school of thoughts Shaivism embraces many theological practices. They all agree on three principles: Pati or God; Pashu or individual soul and Pasa or bonds that confine the soul to earthly existence. The aim of Shaivites is to rid their souls of bondage and achieve Shivata, the "nature of Shiva". They achieve this through ascetic practices and penances, with an emphasis on yoga and renunciation. Many Shaivites become wandering Sadhus or Holy men. Shaivites mark their foreheads with three horizontal marks representing the three aspects of Shiva.

The Shaiva Upanishads consists of 14 minor Upanishads of Hinduism. They are variously dated from the last centuries of the 1st millennium BCE through the 17th century. These extol Shiva as the metaphysical unchanging reality Brahman and the Atman (soul, self). It includes sections about rites and symbolisms related to Shiva. A few texts such as *Atharvashiras Upanishad* mention Rudra. It asserts all gods are Rudra, everyone and everything is Rudra. It says Rudra is the principle found in all things, their highest goal, the innermost essence of all reality that is visible or invisible. The *Kaivalya Upanishad* describes the self-realized man as whom "feels himself only as the one divine essence that lives in all". He identifies his and everyone's consciousness with that of highest Atman within as that of Shiva.

The Shaiva Puranas viz., the Shiva Purana and the Linga Purana, present mythologies, cosmology and pilgrimage (*Tirtha*) associated with Shiva. The Shiva-related Tantra literature composed between the 8th and 11th centuries is regarded in devotional dualistic Shaivism as Sruti. Dualistic Shaiva Agamas viz. Shaiva Siddhanta particularly considers soul within each living being, and Lord Shiva as two separate realities (dualism, *dvaita*). Other Shaiva Agamas teach that these are one reality (monism, *advaita*), and that Shiva is the soul, the perfection and truth within each living being. In Shiva related sub-traditions, there are ten dualistic Agama texts, eighteen qualified monism-cum-dualism Agama texts and sixty four monism Agama texts.

The various dualistic and monist Shiva-related ideas were welcomed in medieval southeast Asia, inspiring numerous Shiva-related temples, artwork and texts in Indonesia, Myanmar, Cambodia, Laos, Vietnam, Thailand and Malaysia, with syncretic integration of local pre-existing theologies.

For the Shaivas, Purusha means Lord Shiva and Prakriti means Divine Energy. However unlike the followers of the concept of *Brahman* the Shaivite do not consider Energy to be the Great Illusion (*Maya*) and hence as illusory. To them the very pervasiveness of Shiva Himself is this movable and unmovable (animate and inanimate) creation. So they cannot be unreal. Based on this concept their path of establishing communion with the Supreme God present in this movable and unmovable creation is based on spiritual love. This appears to be entirely derived from devotion. Although *yoga*, penance and meditation are special features of the spiritual practice of the Shaivite yet undoubtedly devotion unto Lord Shiva has been accorded the prime seat in the populace.

Chapter Ten

Lord Shiva in Puranic Peruse

The worship of Shiva is a pan-Hindu tradition, practiced widely across all of India, Nepal, and Sri Lanka. The Sanskrit word "Shiva" comes from the Shri Rudram Chamakam of the Taittiriya Shakha of the Krishna Yajurveda. The word means auspicious. It is used as an adjective only in the Rig Veda as an attributive epithet for several Rigvedic deities, including Rudra. Other popular names associated with Shiva are Mahadeva, Mahesha, Maheshvara, Shankara, Shambhu, Rudra, Rishikesh [Man of knowledge], Hara, Trilochan, Devendra (meaning Chief of the gods), Neelakanta and Trilokinatha (meaning Lord of the three realms).

Adi Shankara, in his interpretation of the name *Shiva*, opined *Shiva* to have multiple meanings: "The Pure One", or "the One who is not affected by three Gunas of Prakriti (Sattva, Rajas, and Tamas)" or "the One who purifies everyone by the very utterance of His name." Chinmayananda Saraswati has further elaborated: *Shiva* means "the One who is eternally pure" or "the one who can never have any contamination of the imperfection of Rajas and Tamas". Shiva's role as the primary deity of Shaivism is reflected in his epithets *Mahadeva* ("Great god"; *maha* "Great" and *deva* "god"), *Mahesvara* ("Great Lord"; *maha* "great" and i*svara* "lord"), and *Paramesvara* ("Supreme Lord").

One of the Indus Valley seals named by the early excavators of Mohenjo-Daro as Pashu-pati" (Lord of cattle). This is considered as an early manifestation of Lord Shiva and looked like an epithet in the form of a figure, either horned or wearing a horned headdress. It is possibly ithyphallic (especially of a statue or other representation of a deity) figure seated in a posture reminiscent of the Lotus position and surrounded by animals. Lord Shiva is mentioned in the Upanishads. Upanishads are considered the chapters of Vedas with the highest purpose: The purpose of knowing your Atman & the Brahman -The Ultimate Reality. Of the Vedic corpus, they alone are widely known. The Central ideas of the Upanishads are at the spiritual core of Hindus. Lord Shiva is the central theme in Shvetashvatara Upanishad that is embedded in the Yajurveda. In the Shvetashvatara Upanishad He is discussed as the Absolute and Supreme Brahman.

The oldest (dated to the period between 1700 and 1100 BC) surviving text of Hinduism, the Rig Veda mentioned about Lord Rudra, the God of the roaring storm. He is usually portrayed in accordance with the element he represents as a fierce, destructive deity in the form of "The Archer" and the arrow is an essential attribute of Rudra. This name appears in the Shiva Sahasranama. Sanskrit meaning of *'Sarva'* is "to kill" or "to injure", leading to interpretation "The Archer who can kill the forces of darkness", matching the similar attribute given to Lord Shiva. In the *Satarudriya*, some epithets of Rudra, such as Sasipanjara ("Of golden red hue as of flame") and Tivasiati ("Flaming bright"), suggest a fusing of the two deities. Agni is said to be a bull, and Lord Shiva possesses a bull as his vehicle, Nandi. In medieval sculpture, both Agni and the form of Shiva known as Bhairava have flaming hair as a special feature.

The exact figure of Shiva is not well documented. What we know about it today was built up over time by the amalgamation of varied ideas to converge into a composite single figure. Lord Vishnu and Lord Shiva began to absorb countless local cults and deities within their folds. Deities were either taken to represent the multiple facets of the same god. They denoted different forms and appellations by which the god came to be known and worshipped.

Shiva became identified with countless local cults by the sheer suffixing of *Isa* or *Isvara* to the name of the local deity, e.g., Bhutesvara, Hatakesvara, Chandesvara, etc." For an example, assimilation took place in Maharashtra, where a regional deity named Khandoba was a patron deity of farming and herding castes. Khandoba was greatly worshipped in Jejuri in Maharashtra. Khandoba has been assimilated as a form of Shiva himself. He is worshipped in the form of a lingam which is known as Khandoveswar.

Shiva forms a Tantric couple with Shakti, the embodiment of energy, dynamism, and the motivating force behind all action and existence in the material universe. Shakti is his transcendent feminine aspect, providing the divine ground of all being. Shakti manifests in several female deities. Sati and Parvati are the main consorts of Shiva. She is also referred to as Uma, Durga (Parvati), Kali and Chandika. Kali is the manifestation of Shakti in her dreadful aspect. The name Kali comes from Kala, which means darkness, time, death, lord of death. Since Shiva is called Kala, the eternal time, Kali, his consort, also means "Time" or "Death" (as in "time has come"). Various Shakta Hindu cosmologies, as well as Shakta Tantric beliefs, worship her as the ultimate reality or *Brahman*. She is also revered as Bhabatarini (literally "redeemer of the universe"). Kali is represented as the consort of Lord Shiva, on whose body she is often seen standing or dancing. Shiva is the masculine force, the power of peace, while Shakti translates to power, and is considered as the feminine force.

In the Vaishnava tradition, these realities are portrayed as Vishnu and Laxmi, or Radha and Krishna. Both Shiva and Shakti have various forms. Shiva has forms like Yogi Raj (the common image of Him meditating in the Himalayas), Rudra (a wrathful form) and Nataraj (a dancer form). Shiva's dance type the 'Lasya' represents the gentle form of dance associated with the creation of the world, and the 'Tandava' represents the violent and dangerous dance, associated with the destruction of weary world.

Shiva's body is said to consist of five mantras, called the panchbrahmans. This is mentioned in the Panchbrahmans Upanishad. As forms of God, each of these has their own names and distinct iconography. They are Sadyo-Jata; Vamdev; Aghora; Tatpurusa and Ishana. These are represented as the five faces of Shiva. They are associated in various texts with the five elements, the five senses, the five organs of perception and the five organs of action. Lord Shiva himself possesses the character of the fivefold Brahman knowing all things of the phenomenal world as of fivefold character. Hindus believe above fivefold characters are in five of his incarnations (Avatar). They are explained in detail further as below.

1) Sadyo-Jata: Lord Shiva took his first incarnation as Sadyo-Jata when Lord Brahma was engrossed in his deep state of meditation during the nineteenth Kalpa named Shweta Lohit. Lord Brahma gave him the name and lauded him. Later on, from the physique of Sadyo-Jata four of his disciple manifested whose names were Sunand, Nandan, Vishwanandan and Upanandan. All of them were of fair complexion.

2) Namadeva: During the twentieth Kalpa named 'Rakta' the complexion of Lord Brahma turned red while he was engrossed in his meditative state. From his body manifested an entity that also was of red complexion. Lord Brahma named him Namadeva considering him to be the incarnation (Avatar) of Lord Shiva and lauded him. Later on four sons were born to Namadeva, whose names were Viraj, Viwah, Vishok and Vishwabhawan. All of them were of red complexion just like their father Namadeva.

3) Tatpurush: The twenty-first Kalpa on the earth was known as 'Peetavasa'. It was named so because of the apparel of Lord Brahma which was of yellow colours. Lord Brahma's prayer resulted into the manifestation of an effulgent entity. Considering this entity as Lord Shiva, Lord Brahma started chanting the mantras of Shiva Gayatri. After the chanting of the mantras numerous entities manifested who had put on apparels of yellow colour on their body. This way the third incarnation (Avatar) of Shiva popularly known as Tatpurush manifested.
4) Aghoresh: After the Peetavasa Kalpa come the Shiva Kalpa. A black complexioned manifested while Lord Brahma was engrossed in his deep meditative state. Lord Brahma considering this entity as Aghor Shiva started lauded him.

5) Ishana: During the Kalpa named Vishwaroop, manifestations of Saraswati and Ishan Shiva took place. Lord Brahma lauded Ishan Shiva after which four divine entities named Jati, Mundi, Shikhandi and Ardhamundi manifested from Ishan Shiva.

Hindus believe that there are eight famous idols of Lord Shiva. They are Sharva, Bhava, Rudra, Ugra, Bheema, Pashupati, Ishan and Mahadeva. Ten incarnations of Shiva and Shakti (Dash Avatar) are as follows:

1. Shiva as 'Mahakal' and his Shakti as 'Mahakali'.
2. Shiva as 'Tar' and his Shakti as 'Tara'.
3. Shiva as 'Bhubaneswar' and his Shakti as 'Bhuvaneshwari'.
4. Shiva as 'Shodash' or 'Srividdyesh' and his Shakti as 'Shodashi'

5. Shiva as 'Bhairav' and his Shakti as 'Bhairavi'.
6. Shiva as 'Chhinamastak' and his Shakti as 'Chhinamasta'.
7. Shiva as 'Dhoomvan' and his Shakti as 'Dhoomvati'.
8. Shiva as 'Baglamukh' and his Shakti as 'Baglamukhi'.

9. Shiva as 'Matang' and his Shakti as 'Matangi'.

10 Shiva as 'Kamal' and his Shakti as 'Kamala'.

If these ten incarnations of Shiva are worshipped along with his ten Mahavidyas then a person is believed to be attaining salvation.

Mythological mysteries associated with Lord Shiva are endless.

One is about the Origin of Eleven Rudras. Mythological scripts given us to belief that Lord Shiva took birth as eleven Rudras from the womb of Surabhi wife of Kashyap son of Lord Brahma with a purpose. The names of these eleven Rudras were as follows: Kapali, Pingal, Bheem, Virupaksha, Vilohit, Shastra, Ajapaad, Ahirbudhnya, Shambhu, Chand and Bhav. These eleven Rudras fought battles with the demons and killed them. After freeing the universe from the demons the deities were relieved. They worshipped these eleven Rudras to express their gratitude and indebtedness.

Apart from above, mythological scripts gave us to believe that Lord Shiva had taken some other incarnation also. They are as follows:

Ardhnaarishwar Avatar, Nandi Avatar, Sharabh Avatar, Grihapati Avatar, Nilakantha Yaksheshwar Avatar, Durvasha Avatar, Mahesh Avatar, Hanuman Avatar, Brishabh Avatar, Piplaad Avatar, Vishwanath Avatar, Dwijeshwar Avatar, Yatinath Avatar, Krishna Darshan Avatar, Awdhuteshwar Avatar, Bhichhuwarya Avatar, Sureshwar Avatar, Bramhchoti Avatar, Sunatnartak Avatar, Sadhu Avatar, Vibhuashwathama Avatar, Kiraat Avtaar, Dakshinamurthy Avatar and Tripurantaka Avatar. Other traditions regard the sage Agastya, the philosopher Adi Shankara and Ashwatthama as avatars of Shiva. Other forms of Shiva include Virabhadra.

Shiva: Ascetic and Householder

Lord Shiva is depicted as both an ascetic yogi and as a householder, the roles which have been traditionally mutually exclusive in Hindu society. Yogi is one who practices Yoga. When depicted as a yogi, Lord may be shown sitting and meditating. Mahayogi refers to his association with yoga. While Vedic religion was conceived mainly in terms of sacrifice, it was during the Epic period that the concepts of tapas, yoga, and asceticism became more important. The depiction of Shiva as an ascetic sitting in philosophical isolation reflects these later concepts.

Lord Shiva, the ascetic was not ready to enter into the household life. He was happy with His meditation in solitude. It was dangerous to convince Him to get ready for wedding. Kamadeva, the god of desire, put his diligent effort to put the desire in Him for the marriage. Lord Shiva never tolerates that someone try to perturb his meditation. Hence in ferocity he incinerated Kamadeva into ashes. A demon named Tarakasura had a boon that he could not be killed by anyone except the son of Shiva. Tarakasura's atrocity had created the havoc and imbalance in the three worlds. So to kill Tarakasura, there was no option left to Gods rather than getting marriage of Shiva with Parvati to procreate their progenies. With the effort of gods and the stringent penance of Parvati, Shiva got ready to get married with Parvati. Hence Shiva became from ascetic to householder, from Shiva to Shankar. Kartikeya took birth as a son of Shiva and Parvati. He had unrivalled vigour, brawn and valiant. He became the chief of Indra's army and killed Taraksura.

Ganesha, the other son of Shiva and Parvati, has an unrivalled brain, wisdom and intelligence. He has capacity to lead the Gana, he is Prathamesh (to be worshipped first before worshipping any other Gods and Goddesses). Once Shiva became Shankar (Householder), He created a complete family. He Himself is complete; only the complete one has the capacity to create the complete.

Lord Shiva henceforth is depicted as a family man and householder as well in the Hindu society. His epithet Umapati ("The husband of Uma") refers to this idea. Uma in epic literature is known by many names, including the benign Parvati. She is identified with Devi Adi Parashakti or the Divine Mother; Adi Shakti (divine energy) as well as goddesses like Tripura Sundari, Durga, Kamakshi and Meenakshi. The consorts of Shiva are the source of his creative energy. They represent the dynamic extension of Shiva onto this universe. His son Ganesha is worshipped as Lord of Beginnings throughout India and Nepal and as the Remover of Obstacles. Kartikeya is worshipped in South India (especially in Tamil Nadu, Kerala and Karnataka) by the names Subrahmanya, Subrahmanyan, Shanmughan, Swaminathan and Murugan, and in Northern India by the names Skanda, Kumara, or Kartikeya. Shiva is also mentioned in some scriptures to have had daughters like the serpent-goddess Manasa and Ashokasundari. The demons Andhaka and Jalandhara and the god Mangala are considered children of Shiva.

Chapter Eleven

Shiva Lingam – Meaning and the myths

Unlike other Hindu deities including Lord Brahma and Lord Vishnu, the only popular form that Lord Shiva is represented is a lingam. The ovoid shape is a representation of the absolute perfection of Lord Shiva. If anything that is beyond form had to be given form, the lingam would be the closest form to the mystical experience of the absolute perfection of Shiva. Shiva is worshiped in this iconic form of Lingam ever since human worshipping of gods began.

The Sanskrit word '*Lingam*' means *symbol*. Thus the literal meaning of *Shiva Lingam* is the symbol of Shiva. The *Shiva Lingam* represents the Supreme *Shiva,* who is formless. When we see a smoke, we infer the presence of fire. Similarly the moment we see Shiva Lingam we immediately visualize the existence of the *Supreme* Shiva. In the Lingam Purana *we find the* meaning: *"the foremost Lingam which is devoid of colour, taste, hearing, touch etc is spoken of as Prakriti or nature."*

The nature itself is a *Lingam (*or symbol) of Shiva. When we see nature, we infer the presence of its creator – Shiva. Shiva Lingam is the mark of Shiva the creator, the sustainer and the terminator. It also dispels the myth that considers Shiva only as a destructor. Another authentic reference comes from Skanda Purana. Here lingam is clearly indicated as the supreme Shiva from where the whole universe is created and where it finally submerges. The writing in Sanskrit leads to meaning: *"The endless sky (that great void which contains the entire universe) is the*

Linga; the Earth is its base. At the end of time the entire universe and all the Gods finally assimilate in to the eternal icon of Lord Shiva i.e. Linga itself".

Forms of Shiva Lingam

Shiva Lingam is worshiped in two common forms – *Chala* (Moveable) Lingam and *Achala (Non-Moveable or Fixed)* Lingam.

<u>Chala Lingam (Moveable Lingam):</u> The Chala Lingams may be kept in the shrine of one's own home for worship. This is prepared temporarily with materials like sand, clay, dough or rice for worship and dispensed with after the worship. Another form of the Chala Lingams can also be worn on the body as a pendent in the necklace etc. Chala Lingams are often made of quartz, mercury or metals or curved from small stone.

<u>Achala Lingam (Fixed Lingam):</u> Achala or Fixed Lingams are installed in temples and are un-moveable once they are installed. There are rigid rules for Achala Lingams which must be followed. Achala Lingams must be offered prayers at fixed times without fail. Greater sanctity is to be maintained. Usually these Lingams are made of black stones.

Worshipping Shiva Lingam:

According to Hinduism the worship of the lingam originated from the famous hymn in the *Atharva-Veda Samhita* sung in praise of the *Yupa-Stambha*, the sacrificial post. In that hymn, a description is found of the beg)ingless and endless *Stambha* or *Skambha* and it is shown that the said *Skambha* is put in place of the eternal Brahman. There were Yajna (sacrificial) fire, its smoke, ashes, and flames, the *Soma* plant, and the ox that used to carry on its back the wood for the Vedic sacrifice. All these were visualised to conceptualise the brightness of Shiva's body, his tawny matted hair, his blue throat and Shiva riding on the bull. These visualisations in the Yupa Skambha in time gave place to the concept of Shiva-Linga. In the text *Linga Purana*, the same hymn is expanded in the shape of stories, meant to establish the glory of the great Stambha and the superiority of Shiva as Mahadeva.

Jyotirlinga means "The Radiant sign of The Almighty". The Jyotirlingas are mentioned in the *Shiva Purana*. A Jyotirlinga is best described in its entirety as follows:

1. The all-pervading Brahmatmalinga or all-pervading light.
2. In the Taittiriya Upanishad, the twelve Principles of Brahma, Maya, the jiva, the mind, intellect, subconscious mind, ego and the Panchamahabhutas have been referred to as the twelve Jyotirlingas.
3. The twelve sections of the Shivalinga.
4. In the Yajnavedi (Pit where the ritual of sacrificial fires is performed), the shalunka represents the pit of the fire and the linga the flame of the fire.
5. A representation of the twelve Adityas (Species of Deities who are designated into groups).
6. The sites of eruption of fire from the dormant volcanoes.

Since Yama, the master of southern direction is a subordinate of Shankar, south becomes the direction of Shankar. The Jyotirlingas are south-oriented, meaning, the opening of their shalunkas face southwards. Most temples do not face the southern direction. When the opening of the shalunkas faces the south, its pinda possesses more spiritual energy; while the pinda with the opening of the shalunkas facing north possesses lesser energy.

A Jyotirlinga or Jyotirling or Jyotirlingam is a devotional object representing the Supreme God Shiva. *Jyoti* means 'radiance' and *lingam* the 'Image or Sign' of Shiva; *Jyotir Lingam* thus means The Radiant Sign of the Almighty Siva.

The principle Legend associated with the Jyotirlinga is one where Lord Shiva is considered to have appeared for the first time as the endless blazing (Radiant) flame before the other two Lords of the Trinity. The description is available in the Shiva Mahapurana which we have already known. We came to know once Brahma and Vishnu had an argument over supremacy of creation. To settle the debate, Supreme God Shiva pierced the three worlds appearing as a huge Infinite Pillar of Light, the *Jyotirlinga* which later cooled into the Holy Mountain Annamalai (on which the Temple of Arunachaleshvara is located). Vishnu and Brahma split their ways to downwards and upwards respectively to find the end of the light in either direction. Brahma lied that he found out the end, while Vishnu conceded his defeat when Lord Shiva manifested before them. Both realised the prior existence of the superior Supreme Being than both of them. The Jyotirlinga is the form of Supreme Shiva, inseparable reality, out of which Shiva appeared in another Form, Lingodbhava.

Spiritual significance lies in selecting an appropriate Jyotirlinga and the correct Abhishekam (consecration of deities by ritualistic bath with water, milk, etc) on that Jyotirlinga for the proper communication. For example, Mahakaleswar is charged with Tama (one of the three components in the Universe denoting inertia and ignorance) predominant energy. Nagnath is in Harihar form and is Sattva-Tama-predominant and Tryambakeshwar is three components-oriented (also known as Avadhut).

The importance of Jyotirlingas and the place of Samadhi of Saints are complementary. After taking Samadhi, the work of Saints is more at the subtle level. Their bodies emit greater quantum of waves of Chaitanya and sattvikta. Just as the Samadhi of a Saint is under the surface of earth, so also are the Jyotirlingas and Swayambhu Shivalingas. Since these Shivalingas have greater amount of nirguntattva when compared with the other Shivalingas, they constantly emit greater quantum of nirgun Chaitanya and sattvikta. This helps in continuously purifying the atmosphere on the earth. Also, since these waves are constantly emitted towards the region of Hell, they are in continuous combat with the negative energies there. Hence, the earth is constantly protected from the attacks of powerful negative energies from the region of Hell.

Indian Jyothirlinga shrines are Temples where Shiva appeared as a fiery column of light. Originally there were believed to be 64 Jyotirlingas while 12 of them are considered to be very auspicious and holy. Each of the twelve jyothirlinga sites take the name of the presiding deity, each considered a different manifestation of Shiva. In all these sites, the primary image is lingam representing the beginning less and endless Stambha pillar, symbolizing the infinite nature of Shiva.

The twelve Jyotirlinga's are mentioned in the Shiva Purana (Satarudra Samhita, Ch.42/2-4). These shrines are **Somnath** at Prabhas Patan in Kathiawar in Gujarat, **Mallikarjuna** at Srisailam in the Kurnool district of Andhra Pradesh, **Mahakaleshwar** at Ujjain city of Madhya Pradesh, **Omkareshwar** near Barwah in Madhya Pradesh, **Kedarnath** in the Rudra Prayag district of Uttarakhand, **Bhimashankar** at Khed Tehsil in Pune district of Maharashtra, **Viswanath** at Varanasi city in Uttar Pradesh, **Tryambakeshwar** at Tryambak village in Nashik district of Maharashtra, **Vaidyanath** at Deoghar in Madhupur district of

Jharkhand, **Nageshwar Nagnath** at Darukavana in Dwarka in Gujarat, **Rameshwar** at Setubandh at Rameshwaram in Tamil Nadu and **Ghrushneshwar** at Verul village in Aurangabad district of Maharashtra. It is believed that reciting within oneself these names of twelve Jyotirlingas every morning alone purifies one's mind and soul.

Mahadev, the Lord incorporates in Himself, the aura and the holiness of all the twelve Jyotirlingas. The grandeur of these places is unique. Devotees line up in great numbers to take a look and get a Darshan of all the Jyotirlingas. Two on the sea shore, three on river banks, four in the heights of the mountains and three in villages located in meadows, the twelve Jyotirlingas are spread out like this. Every place has been described in glorious words by many detailing the surroundings etc.

Those of us who go to these temples of Lord Shankar-Jyoti-Sivasthan receive the holy blessings of the Lord, and come back happy, peaceful and blessed. This indeed depends on one's devotion and experience too. Those who chant the Dwadasa Jyotirlinga Stotram or prayer will attain salvation and enlightenment and be released from this cycle of human existence with all its travails. By worshipping the Lingas, people of all castes, creeds and colour would be freed from all difficulties.

As a matter of fact, we do the Darshan of the Jyotirlingas as a part of our daily life. Sun, Fire and Light etc., are indeed a part of that great Light. "Om tatsavituvarenye" these magical words of the Gayatri mantra or chant invoke this Supreme light only. By chanting this powerful Mantra, humans can obtain divine power to their life-light or Atmajyothi. The aura of the Sun rays and the various benefits that can be derived there from is indeed a difficult task to describe. This gorgeous life-light is the only thing that is responsible for the activity in the universe. We salute this life force.

"Agni" or fire is a great light. For all the activities on the earth, "Fire" is the pivot. Deepajyoti or light and its greatness are known to all of us and we offer our prayers. Let us celebrate the glory of light. Light is offered a place of pride at welcome celebrations and on all auspicious occasions.

"Shubham karoti kalyanam Arogyam Dhanasampada|
Shatru buddhi vinashaya Deepa Jyoti namostute"

This light removes the darkness from the lives of one and all. Darkness means ignorance and it is destroyed by this light. The natured light of God makes all our wishes come true, when we dip into by taking a Darshan of it. Thus, by taking a Darshan of these twelve Jyotirlingas, the auspicious air surrounding them and the holy pilgrimage, will bring happiness, peace and satisfaction to all.

Jyotirlingas are in a sense minutely different from the temples of the other Hindu deities. Jyotirlingas are not ordinary Shivalinga. They are Swayambhu (appeared on its own) as believed by Hindus. They are created where and whenever Lord Mahadev had to appear on person and provide the solution to save the mankind. Those appearances happen as a result of the people's critical and desperate prayer. Prayer is based on faith and belief in God's ability and leads to the Supernatural rescue event. It is reported in the Hindu Mythology that every Jyotirlingas goes with its own Mythological legends. These legends comprise of the stories goes with Lord Shiva's incarnation or avatars or manifestation or appearance in any form. These manifestations are associated with the local deity or the local person. The noble purpose is to protect the mankind from oppression of asuras, destruction by dishonest but powerful cruel entities, threats of killings & destruction, betrayal and conspiracies, possible debacle and extinction, etc., major happenings in the earth. People in their pursuit of happiness, peace of mind and fulfillment of wishes, believes in such parables and venture into pilgrimage to such cosmic sites.

These particular mysteries with Lord Shiva and its Jyotirlingas have influenced mankind for quite long. I too developed a keen desire to search within these insights of Jyotirlinga and complete my journey within this life. To fulfil this search I have travelled a wide spectrum of my country along with my wife and son from time to time. We collated information during our visits to Jyotirlingas and these have formed the second part of the novel.

> *Like the butter hidden in milk, the Pure Consciousness resides in every being. That ought to be constantly churned out by the churning rod of the mind."*

Part Two

Amidst the Jyotirlings

*[Having learnt about Lord Shiva's place in the Hinduism, I went ahead further to understand to what extent people have been influenced by Lord Shiva in reality. This treatment is based on my actual experience gathered during the pilgrimage undertaken by me along with my family from time to time to all the Twelve Jyotirlingas in India. I have narrated in detail how our visit to the God's shrines opened up with the many sides of reality of people's obedience and reverence for Lord Shiva. We experienced with the realisation that no obstructions what so ever may it be could forbid them from bowing down before their Lord. This unique realisation supplemented with the mythology associated with each of the Jyotirlinga made us to wander from place to place. I could fulfil my intention to complete the pilgrimage to all the twelve Jyotirlinga. This part forms the stories down from our memory lane about our passage through the **Jyotirlings**, the immortal Script, connecting us with the Power of Belief and redefining Human Faith. Walk the Jyotirling thus forms the travelogue]*

Chapter Twelve

Pratham Jyotirlinga Somnath

The period was sometimes in Oct 1994 and place Vadodara (Gujarat).

I was posted there and have spent just five months after coming here on transfer from the previous place of work. My family has always been very eager to travel in new places, see new things, meet and interact with new people. History and mysteries had been favourite subjects of my son. To these are added pilgrimage and nature, favourite topics of me and my wife. Being inquisitive in nature I do not generally skip any such occasion of family trip. So when we sat down to decide that we would spend the Puja holidays in coastal Gujarat region, the idea of visiting Somnath temple stroke my mind. This was our first major excursion trip for 5 days in Gujarat. We decided to cover the travel route as Vadodara-Veraval-Somnath-Chorwad-Junagarh-Vadodara.

Our train reached Veraval Junction in the early morning. After getting refreshed we completed breakfast and opted for sightseeing. With the help of hotel personnel we fixed a local cab to see Somnath temple and the surrounding mythological places.

Somnath is traditionally considered the first sacred pilgrimage site. The Dwadash (Twelve) Jyotirlinga pilgrimage begins with the Somnath Temple. This site at Prabhas Patan in the Gir Somnath district of Gujarat (Saurashtra region) has been a pilgrimage site from ancient times. It is located on the southern corner of the Kathiawar peninsula with its headquarters at the town of Veraval. This place is very close to the famous Triveni sangam (the joining of three rivers viz, Kapila, Hiran and the mythical Sarasvati River).

Geographically the location of the temple is very significant. It is situated at such a place that there is no land in a straight line between Somnath seashore until Antarctica. This information is derived from the Sanskrit inscription found on the Banastambha (literally meaning arrow pillar) erected on the sea-protection wall. The Banastambha mentions that it stands at a point on the Indian landmass that is the first point on land in the north to the South Pole at that particular longitude. This geographical revelation is marvelous – is not it?

In Hinduism, Chandra is a lunar god and a Graha. Chandra is also identified with the Vedic lunar deity *Soma*. The Soma name refers particularly to the juice of sap in the plants, thus making the Moon the lord of plants and vegetation. Chandra is described as young, beautiful, fair; two-armed and having in his hands a club and a lotus. He rides his chariot across the sky every night, pulled by ten white horses or an antelope. He is connected with dew, and as such, is one of the gods of fertility. He is also called Rajanipati and Indu.

According to Prabhaskhand of Skanda Purana in the Hindu Mythology, the legend goes like this: Chandra has not been very fortunate in life. Chandra was born in the Ocean of Milk, and nearly blinded the gods with his bright, glowing body. The gods unanimously decided to give Chandra the status of a planet and sent him into the cosmos. Chandra had a series of disastrous love affairs. His first lover, Tara, was the wife of Brihaspati (the planet Jupiter). From their union, Tara gave birth to Budha. Because of this illegitimate relationship both Budha and his father Chandra began to hate each other and their rivalry continues to this day. For the sin of abducting another god's consort, Brahma banished Chandra to the outer atmosphere. Thus Chandra was no more a planet. This story illustrates allegorically the prohibition of intoxicants for Brahmins. After that, Chandra, set out to marry the twenty-seven daughters of Daksha. Daksha allowed this on the condition that the Moon should not favor any daughter over the others. Chandra failed to follow this as he was partial to Rohini, his favorite and neglected the others. The remaining twenty six wives felt neglected and insulted. Being disappointed with their husband they complained to their father. Daksha was extremely annoyed and cursed Chandra to wane into nothingness. The curse took away his luster. The Devas (Celestial gods) were very sad at Chandra's plight. They went to Lord Brahma and prayed to find out a remedy for this condition of Chandra and to get a solution for redressing the curse. Brahma told them to worship Vrishabhdhwaj Shankar at Prabhas Kshetra Mahamrityunjay (Shiva in the previous aeons was referred to as Mrityunjaya or Kalabhairava or Bhairavanatha at Somnath).

A disturbed Chandra came down to Prabhasa with wife Rohini. He went on a severe penance and worshipped the Sparsa Linga of Somnath. Mention of the Sparse Linga of Somnath as one bright as the sun, the size of an egg, lodged underground, is available in the Skanda Purana. Thus the Legend confirms that the Kalabhairava Shivalinga (Bhairavanatha) at Prabhasa was worshipped by God Chandra (the moon). Pleased with Chandra's worship Lord Shiva appeared before him and blessed him with boon that in a month he would grow for fifteen days in one half and in the other half he would keep losing one Kala (shade) per day and decrease in size. He was pleased with the Devas. As Lord Shiva appeared here before Soma or Moon God and rescued him from Daksha's curse, the Jyotirlinga here represents the manifestation of Lord Shiva as Somnath. The Devas established a Kund there known as Someshwar. Hindus believe a holy dip in this Kund releases one from all the sins. It is believed that Lord Brahma installed the Brahmasila and paved the way for the construction of the temple by the Moon God who is believed to have installed the Golden Jyotirlinga. As Chandra got back his original brightness or Prabhas here, this place became famous as "Prabhasapattana".

Available historical evidences could not conclude the exact time period of the construction of this Shrine. News of the Shrine's enormous wealth, rich ornamented construction and the prosperity associated with this legendary temple reached far flung countries. As a result the temple has been the target for plundering, loot and destruction by many Islamic rulers and Portuguese invaders. There had been invasion as many as sixteen times in the past since its first construction. While the first attack was said to be by the Sindh Subedar Junaid in 722 AD, the final horrible destruction, plunder and loot was conducted by a few blacksheeps amongst the Mughals during Aurangzeb's reign in 1701 AD. The most resilient factor of Hinduism is noted with great reverence that after each loot and destruction the temple was rebuilt from time to time by the Hindu kings. As per available information the second temple was said to have built at the same site by the Seuna kings or Yadavas of Devagiri, while the third time the temple was constructed by Gurjara-Pratihara king Nagabhata II which was a large structure of red sandstone. In 1783 AD Rani Ahilya Devi Holkar, a great devotee of Shiva, built a new temple for Somanath. Most recently it was rebuilt in November 1947, when Vallabhbhai Patel visited the area for the integration of Junagadh with Indian Govt and mooted a plan for restoration.

The temple in the present form which we visited was reconstructed after our independence under the supervision of one Mr K M Munshi, the then Central Minister by collecting funds, donations from public on the advice of Mahatma Gandhi. Dr. Rajendra Prasad, the First President of Independent India performed the installation ceremony for the temple in May 1951. The President said in his address, "The Somnath temple signifies that the power of reconstruction was always greater than the power of destruction".

The temple remains open daily from 6AM to 9PM. There are 3 Aarti daily; in the morning at 07:00, at 12:00 and in the evening at 19:00. We were lucky to attend the noon Aarti and completed our darshan with great Reverence and Bhakti. The inner temple or the Garbhagriha was aglow with the luster of many gemstones. The Shiva linga in the temple was believed to be safely hide within its hollowness of the famous Syamantak Mani, the Philosopher's stone associated with Lord Krishna. It was a magical stone, capable of producing gold. It is believed that this stone had alchemic and radioactive properties. It could create a magnetic field around itself that kept the linga floating above ground. King was amazed by the marvel of the idol that it stayed in the air without prop or support. He enquired about the reason. Initially it was thought that it was upheld by some hidden support. The king directed a person to go and feel all around and above and below it with a spear, which he did, but met with no obstacle. One of the attendants came out with a logical answer. He stated that the canopy was made of lodestone (a naturally magnetized mineral; magnetite) and the idol of iron. The inventive builder had skillfully contrived that the magnet should not exercise a greater force on any one side – hence the idol was suspended in the middle. When two stones were removed from the summit, the idol swerved on one side; when more were taken away, it inclined still further, until at last it rested on the ground. Perhaps that is why the statue of Somnath always appears to be at the center because of the miraculous magnetic power. The Nanda Deep was always kept lighted with Kannauji attar.

The temple had vast wealth. For worship of the Lord and for Abhishekam sandalwood scented water brought from Haridwar is said to be used. Flowers for special festivities are said to be brought from Kashmir. It is once said that for the routine daily worship initially a thousand Brahmins were appointed. This rich religious place of worship is believed to have received the produce of ten thousand nearby villages.

Somnath Jyotirlinga

Among the twelve Jyotirlingas Somnath is considered as the primary one. The deity is said to be Swayambhu (self-born) and is always awake. Lakhs of devotees visit this temple. They consider themselves blessed and have achieved piety. Offerings made by crores of devotees have made the Somnath Temple rich.

Photography was not allowed inside the temple. So a scanned copy of the picture of the sanctorum is shown above. Below is shown the picture which we took from the outside of the temple.

Somnath Temple from the Sea-beach side

After paying our obedience and reverence to Lord Shiva we stood there for a few minutes. We felt for a second in the peace and tranquility that we were in the midst of an unattached world. Then we came out of the Jyotirling Shrine and roamed around for a while in the temple courtyard.

Later on we ventured into nearby sightseeing. It covered the Bhalka Teerth at a distance of 5 km, a Holy Hindu pilgrimage site. It is said that Lord Vishnu was killed here when he was seating on a huge banyan tree branch totally dejected after seeing his brother Balaram's entry into Samadhi. From there we were taken to the Triveni Sangam Ghat. This is also a very sacred place in the Hindu Mythology and Puranas and finds a mention in the Hindu epics Ramayana and Mahabharata. This is the confluence of three rivers - Kapila, Hiran and a mystical River Saraswati, which are believed to be flowing to their ultimate destination – Arabian Sea, representing three stages of human life- human birth, life and death. It is said that Lord Krishna left his earthly body at this place. A holy dip at this Ghat gets one rid of all curses and diseases. We also found two more temples located on the banks of the Ghat – they were popular temples Gita Mandir and Lakshminarayan temple. From there we further moved to the west and visited the Goddess Chandrabhaga Shaktipeeth, locally known as Kali Mandir.

Then it was time to return to our hotel at Veraval for lunch and rest.

When we think now, we feel it was a miracle that we unknowingly visited Somnath temple, the Pratham Jyotirlingam to start our Jyotirling pilgrimage. Subsequently we visited all the remaining eleven Jyotirlingas. It was as if Lord Shiva himself set our itinerary. Today we feel very happy and satisfied.

Chapter Thirteen

Path to Moksha - Vishveshwar

That was Dec 1998. I was posted at Kanpur. We were planning to spend a few holidays in Varanasi and Allahabad.

As the name of Varanasi came up immediately my thoughts turned to the fact that Vishveshwar Mahadev, one of the 12 Shiva Jyotirlingas was situated there. That was how our visit to second Jyotirlinga took place.

We took an evening train Chauri Chaura Express from Kanpur and reached Varanasi in the mid- night. We straightway checked in a nearby hotel booked earlier. As per plan next morning a friend of mine came and took us to have Darshan of Vishveshwar Jyotirlinga at Kashi Vishwanath temple.

Located on the banks of the holy river the Ganges, Varanasi in Uttar Pradesh is regarded among the holiest of the Hindu cities. Name Varanasi is said to be derived from the names of the two rivers the Varuna and the Ashi that flowed through the city. Kashi Vishwanath Temple, one of the most famous Hindu temples dedicated to Lord Shiva is located here. The temple stands on the western bank of the river Ganga and is one of the twelve Jyotirlingas, the holiest of Shiva temples. The main deity is known by the name Vishwanath or Vishveshwar meaning *Ruler of the Universe*. The Varanasi city is also called *Kashi,* and hence the temple is popularly come to know as Kashi Vishwanath Temple.

We reached at the Vishwanath temple gate and get down from our car. We walked through a small lane called the Vishwanath Galli around which on both sides there were many smaller shrines. Close to the temple entry gate there was a flower shop where we kept our shoes and washed our hands. We purchased flowers and necessary offerings to be made from the shop and entered the temple complex on bare foot. Our feet got continuously cleaned by the flowing water on the temple floor. As per the structure of the temple, there was a Sabha Gruh or congregation hall where we stood in a Queue for darshan. After sometime the line led us to the inner Garbha Gruh or Sanctum. We entered the Garbha Gruh and bowed our head before the Lord Vishveshwar Mahadev. When our turn came we offered our flowers and leaves and prayer to the Lord with utmost devotion and reverence. The kind priest allowed us to touch the Linga as well. The venerable linga is made up of black colored stone of about 60 cm tall and 90 cm in circumference housed in a square alter. After offering our prayer to the Lord Mahadev we came out of the Garbha Gruh and took a parikrama round the temple.

Structure of the temple as we found from outside consisted of three parts. The first comprised a 15.5 metre high gold spire, the second was gold dome and the third was the gold spire atop the Vishwanath carrying a flag and a trident. There were three domes each made up of pure gold. The main temple was quadrangle and was surrounded by shrines of other gods. There were small temples for Kalabhairava, Dhandapani, Avimukteshwara, Vishnu, Vinayaka, Sanishwara, Virupaksha and Virupaksh Gauri in the complex.

After completing our round in the complex we walked down the adjacent premise where we found a small well to the north of the main temple. This was called the *Gyaan vapi* (the wisdom well). There was a Mosque located adjacent to the well in the same compound heavily protected through layers of tall iron grills. It is believed that the Jytorlinga was hidden in the well to protect it at the time of Muslim invasion. It was learnt that the then main priest of the temple jumped in this well along with the Shiva Linga in order to protect the Jyotirlinga from the invaders.

The Vishveshwar Jyotirling has a very special and unique significance in the spiritual profile of India. Many leading saints, including Adi Sankaracharya, Ramakrishna Paramhansa, Swami Vivekananda, Goswami Tulsidas, Swami Dayananda Saraswati and Gurunanak have visited the site. As per the Hindu Mythology, the legend has it: The mother of Goddess Parvati once felt ashamed that her son-in-law had no decent dwelling. Lord Shiva understood this and desired Varanasi as the spot as his Royal residence. To please Parvati, Shiva with the help of his disciple demon Nikumbha (son of Kumbhakarna) arranged suitable dwelling place at Kashi. Thus Kashi became his winter residence on the plains. One occasion Shiva left Kashi for some reasons. The gods were afraid that Kashi would lose its reverence if it was not properly managed. So they called for help of Lord Brahma.

Concerned Brahma after a long search for a solution found a sage of royal blood performing hard tapas in the jungle near the city of Kashi. The sage in deep meditation was Prince Ripunjay. Satisfying with his penance Brahma appeared before him. Devoted prince bowed to Lord Brahma. Brahma gently said "Oh man of high soul! Time has come when you should bear the crown, rule the world and reform dharma". Ripunjay listened calmly and fathom the offer made by the Lord. Being independent minded, he spoke, "My lord, I shall happily do what you command but on one condition that I be allowed to rule without intervention. In peace I could reform the dharma. I wish all Gods and Godly entities to not set feet upon my land and remain away from my land." "So be it" said Brahma but not before Brahma got King agreed in return that he would be an excellent administrator and all residents staying in his kingdom would be treated well with proper religious pursuits. On the command of Brahma, all Gods left to the heaven.

Ripunjay was then renamed to King Divodasa. He took the throne and worked vigorously to bring order in the decaying world. He established a rule so flawless that was never seen before. Under his reign, his subjects prospered and justice flourished.

As time passed, Lord Shiva desired to again come back to his own city Kashi. But due to Brahma's boon to Divodasa, he was unable to set feet in Kashi. Soon Lord Shiva came to know that other gods too are unable to stay in his city. Not happy with this kind of attitude of the King Divodasa, Lord Shiva came out with a plan to end Divodasa's reign.

Shiva first sent messengers. They came and loved the city so much that they didn't go back. Then he sent sixty Yoginis on the advice of his wife Goddess Parvati to Kashi for disrupting the perfectness of Divodasa's rule. The Yoginis too were overwhelmed with the city's perfectness and settled there itself instead. Lord Shiva then sent God Surya to Kashi. But once Suryadev saw the Kashi city he also fell in love with it and turning south tilted to one side and settled down there.

Then Shiva sent Brahma. When his persuasion failed Brahma entered Kashi in the guise of a Sadhu. Soon he had the king under his influence. He advised the King Divodasa to arrange an Ashwamedha Yagna with ten horses. He did it to ensure failure of the Yagna. King's army divided in ten parts and followed ten horses. To Brahma's dismay, all horses came back safely with their armies. Lord Brahma was too ashamed of the failure of his trickery. Shiva unable to trust anyone then deputed two of his most trusted ganas. But they loved the place very much. They thought this would be the only place Shiva should live and so they stayed there and became Dwarapalakas of this city.

Failing in all his efforts enhanced further his desire to go to Kashi city. He approached Lord Vishnu who laid out a scheme. As per this plan Ganesh arrived at Kashi in the disguise of an astrologer. Ganesh established his residence near the city and began serving the citizens as astrologer. Fame of the astrologer spread in the kingdom. Touched by wind of the fame, the queen also sought his service and was impressed by the astrologer. Soon Ganesh as astrologer found place in the royal court of the king. In the pretext of reading his palm, Ganesh could convince the King that in spite of having everything in Kashi still he had no mental peace. He informed that a holy and wise Sage would come to see the king on the eighteenth day. Council of the wise man would bring wealth of enlightenment.

Lord Vishnu came in disguise of the saint and told the king "Undoubtedly you are the one who established law of dharma on the earth again and saved it. But just one deed of yours to ask Shiva to leave his beloved city is cursing your mental peace. By no means is your deed right. You need to correct it by making a Shiv Linga & worship him to come to his city Anandavan. Lord Vishnu as Saint said to king that on the 7th day after installation of Shiva linga, a celestial plane will appear and grant moksha to the king by carrying him to Lord Shiva's abode. The Shivalinga installed was named after the king as Divodaseswara Shiva. Thus Lord Vishnu caused the departure of King Divodasa and gave Varanasi back to Lord Shiva. Lord Siva once again appeared there and decided to reside there permanently. Along with wife Devi Parvati once again he started blessing his devotees with wonderful boons.

There is Goddess Parvati's Shrine adjacent to Lord Vishwanath Shrine. It is believed pleased Devi Parvati offered food (Annam) to one and all. Hence Goddess Parvati is worshipped as Annapurna. The Lord Shiva himself came with a bowl in his hands asking for Annam from the seated Devi at the Parvati's shrine. This is considered to be one of the 51 Shaktipeeths. We also visited this great shrine.

There are legends in air that the true devotee achieves freedom from death and saṃsara by the worship of Vishveshwar here. It is believed Shiva's devotees on death are being directly taken to his abode on Mount Kailash by his messengers and not by Yama. There is a popular belief that Shiva himself blows the mantra of salvation into the ears of people who die naturally at the Vishwanath temple. This is the high significance of this Jyotirlinga. Hindus from all over the world try to visit the place at least once in their lifetime to lead one on a path to Moksha (liberation).

The temple has been mentioned in the Puranas including the Kashi Khanda of Skanda Purana. Varanasi thus became an eyesore and source of jealousy for many including the Muslims. From 1033 to 1669 AD starting with Qutb-ud-din Aibak in 1194 CE up to Mughal Emperor Aurangzeb in 1669 AD, Kashi came under several destructive attacks. Temples were demolished and Masjids built there instead. But due to the dedication of the Hindu devotees, the Jyotirlinga survives and remained the greatest Hindu pilgrimage place. During the reign of the British and the Marathas, this place further developed.

The Kashi Vishveshwar temple as we see it now was built by Malhar Rao's daughter-in-law Ahilyabai Holker in 1780 AD. It was built in adjacent to the mosque built by Aurangzeb earlier. In

1828 AD, Baija Bai, widow of the Maratha ruler Daulat Rao Scindhia of Gwalior State, built a low-roofed colonnade with as many as 40 pillars. This is known as the Gyan Vapi precinct which is visible today. During 1833-1840 CE, the boundary of Gyanvapi Well, the ghats and other nearby temples were constructed by many noble families from various ancestral kingdoms of India. In 1841 AD, the Bhonsle of Nagpur donated silver to the temple. In 1859 AD, Maharaja Ranjit Singh donated 1 tonne gold for plating the temple's tower and dome. A huge bell hangs in the temple. It was donated by the King of Nepal. The temple is being managed by a hereditary group of pandas or mahants presently lead by the family members of Head Priest Pandit Vishveshwar Dayal Tewari.

After offering our prayer with great reverence we took a round in the entire temple complex before coming out. Then we had our breakfast at the nearby restaurant. After having breakfast we roamed around places which included other important temples nearby, tapobhoomi, Dashashwamedh Ghat. Through most part of our passage on foot we heard the chartings viz., *Jaya Ganga, Jaya Vishwanath, and Om Namah Shivaya.*

The chants continued to echo in our ears for long time!!!

Chapter Fourteen

Colossal Fury Mahakaleswar

We were at Indore at that time and had already spent over three years there.

That was the month of October. Our son came to spend his semester vacation with us. We sat down to decide the place for a quick sightseeing.

Two of the twelve Jyotirlingas viz, The Mahakaleshwar Mahadev and the Omkareshwar Mamaleshwar Mahadev were situated close by within 150 km range (to and fro) from Indore. Two temples were however situated in opposite direction to each other. So we decided to visit one of them this time. We decided to have Mahakaleswar Mahadev darshan first.

Mahakaleswar Jyotirlinga is situated in Ujjain which is about 65 Km from Indore. We hired a local cab for a day's sightseeing trip and started for Ujjain.

City of Ujjain also known as Ujjayini or Avantikapuri was the capital of the Avanti kingdom. It is traditionally exalted as one of the seven sacred cities (Sapta Puri) of the Hindus. It is one of the four sites that host the Kumbh Mela (also called the Simhastha Mela), a quadrennial mass pilgrimage that attracts millions of Hindu pilgrims from around the country. In Indian mythology, the origin of the city is ascribed to the act of Sagar Manthan, which refers to the churning of the primordial ocean performed by the demigods and demons to discover a pot containing the nectar of immortality. The Legend goes that after the nectar was discovered a fierce struggle ensued between the demigods and the demons to grab the nectar for the attainment of immortality. During the chase, a drop of nectar spilled and fell on Ujjain, thus making the city sacred. According to legend, the river Kshipra that flows across Ujjain is regarded to have originated owing to the churning of the gods and goddesses. Ujjain is situated on the eastern bank of the Shipra River. Shipra River is considered as a sacred river in Hinduism.

Mahakaleshwar temple is situated on the side of the River Shipra in the city of Ujjain. There is also a large lake named *Rudra Sagar* situated just back of the temple. The temple is protected from the lake by a huge walled boundary. The presiding deity, Lord Shiva in the lingam form is believed to be Swayambhu, deriving currents of power from within itself as against the other images and lingams that are ritually established and invested with mantra-shakti.

Driver parked the taxi in the stipulated parking place. We walked down the street leading to the temple. From outside we found that the Shikhar or the Spire was adorned with sculptural finery. Through a very long zigzag fenced passage outside in the large open courtyard surrounded by massive walls safeguarding from the adjacent lake, we entered into the main temple.

We started stepping down the stairs case through a very dark and narrow passage. Brass Lamps light the way of the devotees to the underground sanctum. We found that the idol of Mahakaleshwar was facing the south direction. We were told that was a unique feature, upheld by the tantric Shivnetra tradition to be found only in Mahakaleshwar among the 12 Jyotirlingas. The images of Ganesh, Parvati and Kartikeya are installed in the west, north and east of the sanctum sanctorum. To the south is the image of Nandi, the vehicle of Lord Shiva. The idol of Nagchandreshwar on the third storey is open for darshan only on the day of Nag Panchami. The temple has five levels, lowest one of which is this underground where we were standing.

According to the Puranas, the city of Ujjain or Avantikapuri was famous for its beauty and prosperity and its status as a devotional epicenter. It was also one of the primary cities where students went to study the Holy Scriptures. According to legend, there was a ruler of Ujjain called Chandrasena. He was a pious devotee of Lord Shiva and worshiped him all the time. One day, a farmer's boy named Shrikhar was walking on the grounds of the palace and heard the King chant the Lord's name and rushed to the temple to start praying with him. However, the guards removed him by force and sent him to the outskirts of the city near the river Kshipra. Rivals of Ujjain, primarily King Ripudamana and King Singhaditya of the neighboring kingdoms decided to attack his Kingdom and take over its treasures around this time. Startled by this news feared Shrikhar started to pray. The news spread to the Brahmin priest named Vridhi who had four sons, who were all devotees of Siva. Shocked on hearing this, they all started to pray to Lord Shiva at the river Kshipra. The Kings chose to attack with the help of the powerful demon Dushan. He was blessed by Lord Brahma to become invisible at his wishes. Together they plundered the city and attacked all the devotees of Lord Shiva. The wicked demon Dushan started torturing the erudite Brahmans. But the Brahmans who were very engrossed in their worship of Shiva did not even flinch. The demon sent all four of his henchmen with the orders that they had to ensure that no Vedic Dharmanushtan activities took place. The harassed people came running to the Brahmans seeking help. The Brahmans assured the people and pacified them. They immediately started praying to Lord Shiva. The heartfelt pleas of His helpless devotees did reach Lord Shiva. When Demon Dushan tried to attack the Brahmans, the earth split open near the Parthiv Murty with a loud noise and forming a huge crater. In this manner, Siva assumed the colossal form of Mahakal and appeared. He warned the wicked Demon to refrain from going anywhere near the Brahmans. But the wicked Demon did not pay heed. Angered Siva appeared in his Mahakal form and burnt him to ashes with just one grunt. He then destroyed the enemies of King Chandrasena. Seeing Lord Siva in this Avatar, Lord Brahma, Lord Vishnu and God Indra and other Devas came down and prayed to the Lord and pacified Him. Upon the request of his devotees

Shrikhar and Vridhi, Lord Shiva agreed to reside in the city. He was made the chief deity of the Kingdom to take care of it against its enemies and to protect all His devotees.

From that day on, Lord Shiva resided in His light form as Mahakala in a Lingam that was formed on its own from the powers of the Lord and His consort, Parvati. The Lord blessed his devotees and declared that people who worshipped Him in this form would be free from the fear of death and diseases. Also, they would be granted worldly treasures and be under the protection of the Lord himself. Lord Vishnu declared that Lord Shiva would thus be worshiped here as Mahakaleshwar Mahadev henceforth.

The presiding deity of time, Shiva, in his entire splendor, reigns eternally in the city of Ujjain. The temple of Mahakaleshwar, its *Shikhar* soaring into the sky, an imposing facade against the skyline, evokes primordial awe and reverence with its majesty. The Mahakal dominates the life of the city and its people and provides an unbreakable link with ancient Hindu traditions.

History: The temple complex was destroyed by Sultan Shas-ud-din Iltutmish during his raid of Ujjain in 1234 AD -1235 AD. The present structure was built by the General of Shrimant Peshwa Baji Rao and Chatrapati Shahuji Maharaj of the Hindu Pad Padshahi--- Shrimant Raanojirao Shinde Maharaj (Scindia) in 1736 AD. Further developments and management was done by Madhavrao Scindia the First (1730 AD–1794 AD) and Shrimant Maharani Bayzabai Raje Scindia (1827–1863). In the regime of Maharaja Shrimant Jiyajirao Scindia until 1886 AD, major programs of the then Gwalior Riyasat used to be held at this Mandir. After Independence the Devasthan Trust was replaced by the municipal corporation of Ujjain. Nowadays it is under the administrative jurisdiction of the Ujjain District collectorate office.

Chapter Fifteen

Narmada Arghya Omkareshwar

It was in one of those Aprils during our stay at Indore, Madhya Pradesh.

Son came home at the end of the semester but for a short period. During the dinner time we were discussing the idea of spending a day on the outskirt of Indore.

As my interest lies in mythology so I raised that we should visit the Omkareshwar Mahadev this time. My wife and son agreed to my proposal. We decided to visit the Omkareshwar Mahadev Jyotirlinga. This was the fourth Jyotirlinga that we visited.

We hired a local cab for a full-day trip to cover visits of Omkareshwar Mahadev and Maheshwar (another Historical site).

Omkareshwar a Hindu temple dedicated to God Shiva is one of the 12 revered Jyotirlinga shrines. Omkareshwar is a beautiful self manifest (Swayambhu) linga. From the Vindhyachal mountain range in Madhya Pradesh River Narmada turns westward and meanders in that direction. The river is deep and wide here. This river Narmada, which flows rippling from the mountains, is also known as "Reva". The smooth, round pebbles found in this river are called "Banalingas". *"Narmada ke Kankar, UtteShankar"* is the belief of the devotees. That is how, Narmada is also known as "Shankari" river.

On the banks of river Narmada, there is a huge island known as Mandhata. This island is formed by the river Narmada branching itself in two parts at the beginning of the island and forming a confluence at the end of the island with the river the

Kaveri. Thereafter it continues to flow as one River Narmada. The island comprises two lofty hills and is divided by a valley in such a way that it appears in the shape of the sacred Hindu symbol 'Om' from above. It is a natural phenomenon.

Between the precipitous hills of the Vindhyachal on the North and the Satpura on the South, the Narmada forms a deep silent pool which in early times was full of alligators and fish, so tame as to take grain from human hand. This pool is 270 ft below the cantilever type bridge constructed later in 1979. The bridge has enhanced the scenic beauty of the place, making it look exceedingly picturesque.

The Narmada banks and the island are extremely beautiful. The beauty of Nature here is seen to be believed. The Island has houses perched on the terraced green, black stone mountains, Koti Teerth, waterfalls, green forests and valleys like Chakra Teerthas. When the devotees go round the mountain valley and island by boating actually they do Parikrama or Circumambulation of Omkara itself. The temple is situated on this island. The temple towers look bright and shiny in between. The whole atmosphere echoes with the sound of "Om Namah Shivaya". It is here that Lord Shiva has taken the forms of "Omkareshwar" and "Amaleshwar" as JyotirLinga.

Omkareshwar Jyotirlinga also has its own history and stories. Three of them are prominent. The first story is about Vindhya Parvat (Mount). According to a legend, once upon a time Narada (Mind son of Lord Brahma), known for his non-stop cosmic travel, visited Vindhya parvat. He paid a visit to the deity of the Vindhya Mountains. He was angry to find that there was no dwelling here suitable for Lord Shiva. In his spicy way Narad told Vindhya Parvat about the greatness of Mount Meru. This made

Vindhya jealous of Meru and he decided to be bigger than Meru. Vindhya started worship of Lord Shiva to become greater than Meru. Vindhya Parvat practiced severe penance and worshipped parthivlinga (A linga made from physical material) along with Lord Omkareshwar for nearly six months. Lord Shiva was pleased and blessed him with his desired boon. Lord Shiva was so pleased that he decided to make Omkareshwar one of his homes. On a request of all the gods and the sages Lord Shiva made two parts of the lingams. One half is called Omkareshwar and the other Mamaleshwar.

Lord Shiva gave Vindhya the boon of growing, but took a promise that Vindhya would never be a problem to Shiva's devotees. Vindhya did not keep his promise and began to grow. It even obstructed the sun and the moon. All deities approached sage Agastya for help. On his way to pilgrimage to south Agastya along with his wife came to Vindhya and convinced him that he would not grow until the sage and his wife returned. But they never returned and Vindhya remained there as it was when they left. The sage and his wife stayed in Srisailam which is regarded as Dakshina Kashi and one of the Dwadash Jyotirlinga.

Another version of mythology associated with this place goes: In the ancient times the Demons defeated the gods making the king of Gods Indra worried. The Demons have wrecked havoc in all the three worlds, i.e., Trilokas. In order to empower the Devas once again, Lord Shiva assumed the form of Jyotirmaya Omkararoop. He came out in the form of Linga on the banks of the river Narmada. Devas worshipped the Linga which made them powerful once again. This time they were able to destroy the demons and recovered their empire in Heavens. Brahma and Vishnu also lived in the same place as Omkar Amaleshwar. That is why on the banks of Narmada Brahmapuri, Vishnupuri and

Rudrapuri are built which are known as Tripuri Kshetra. The Amareshwar JyotirLinga is situated in Rudrapuri.

As per the third mythological era or Purana Kala, *Yavanaswa Putra Mandhata* came into power here with the blessings of Indra. He served Lord Shankara with great devotion. Lord Shankara was pleased with him. The waters of Narmada emanated as the Arghya (holy water) of the Omkar JyotirLinga and flew through the mountains, downward and later on into an unseen flow. Narmada joins the deep-water spring located near the Linga idol of Omkareshwar. It flows there eternally. When some bubbles appear at the bottom of this spring, it is said, that Lord Shankar is pleased. King Mandhata made this holy place his capital. Therefore, this place is also known as Omkar Mandhata. The descendents of Mandhata live here even today. The whole place turned beautiful. Many hermits like Agastya have performed severe penances and japas at Omkareshwar-Amaleshwar JyotirLinga. They had built their hermitages.

This place of pilgrimage became famous in the historical times too. In 1063 AD, Parmar king Udayaditya installed four stone inscriptions with four Sanskrit Stotras and dedicated them to the Amaleshwar Temple. Pushpadanta's "Shiva Mahima Stotra" can also be seen as a stone inscription.

Initially aboriginals used to live here on Omkareshwar Island as a settlement. It belonged to Kalika Devi. Devotees of this goddess known as Bhairavgan, used to harass pilgrims. They used to sacrifice them. After sometime, a saint by the name Dariyayinath took charge of that place and stopped the atrocities of the Bhairavgan. Since then, pilgrims started moving there freely. After that, Bhil reign began there. In 1195 AD, King Bharat Singh Chauhan won over the Bhils and improved the grandeur of the

Omkar Mandhata. Even today the palace ruins of Raja Bahrat Singh Chauhan can be seen.

The temple was renovated by Peshwa Baji Rao II. Later Maharani Ahilya Devi Holkar made several improvements in this ancient shrine. She built beautiful ghats. Guru Shankaracharya is believed to have said "I pay my obeisance to the One who is the savior of the good people and the great One Who always resides at the Holy merging point of Kaveri and Narmada, i.e., Omkareshwar Mahadev".

From the parking place we walked down the road leading to the bridge built over the Narmada River. After crossing the bridge we took a right turn and walked through the temple lane. On both side of this lane there are shops selling varieties of beautiful local show pieces made from black stones. Finally we reached temple courtyard. There is a long stare case that took us to the upper level from where we entered the temple inside. This is the temple part said to contain the Omkareshwar Jyotirlinga. We reached the Garbhagriha and paid our reverence to the Lord. Lord Shiva is said to have manifested here on the prayer of the oppressed people in two different levels. We then climbed up further through the stare case from behind this temple to top of the hills.

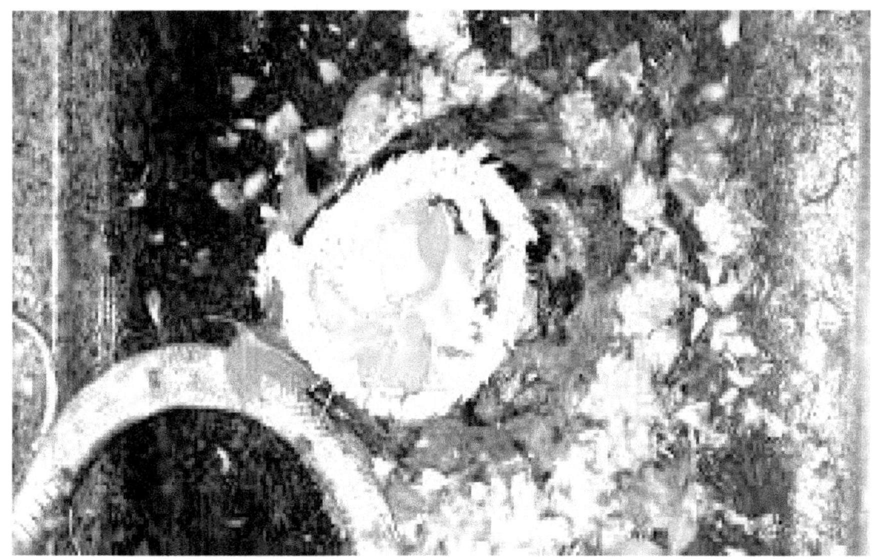

This temple contains the Mamaleshwar Jyotirling. Omkareshwar temple is closely associated with Mamaleshwar temple, as both these temples are deemed as single form of Lord Shiva. It is said that the temple of Mamaleshwar holds the actual Jyotirlinga although Omkareshwar Temple being famous for the Jyotirlinga. The Mamaleshwar Temple is a temple with a hall and a sanctum. The Shiva Linga is present in the centre of sanctum. An idol of Goddess Parvati is located on the backside of the Shiva Linga, in the wall. We offered our prayers to the Lord. We then got protection thread (kalaba) put on our wrist by the priest. Paying our reverence and bhakti we completed our Darshan. Then we roamed around the temple complex. The temple is said to be built in the Nagara style of architecture, with fine carvings. This is like a cave said to have in existence since thousands of years. We took a few pictures of the temple from the foot bridge on the Narmada.

Finishing our Jyotirlinga darshan we proceeded to Maheshwar which was about 55 km from there. We reached

Maheshwar town in about 45 min. First we completed our lunch at a roadside restaurant.

Next we reached the Maheshwar Fort, an old Historical palace of the Holkars, located on the bank of the river Narmada. The scenic beauty of the place along with the old Shiv Mandir established by Maharani Ahilyabai Holkar created a very sublime reverence and serenity in the place. We enjoyed our stay in the fort complex. After about an hour we started our return journey for Indore.

Chapter Sixteen

Protector Nagnath Nageshwar

That was the month of December. We were staying at Indore.

Five days week has just been implemented in our company. In a celebration mood we planned to visit Dwarka in the coastal Gujarat in the second week. The route was chosen as Indore-Vadodara-Dwarka-Vadodara-Indore. Vadodara was included in the itinerary merely as an intermediate station for catching the connecting train to Dwarka.

Our train Okha Exp reached Dwarka in the morning. We had booked our accommodation in Dwarka Toran (a GTDC Hotel). Auto took us there comfortably through Dwarka roads. We had the glimpse of the calm and quite Dwarka both fell in love with the place instantly.

After completing our check in formalities I enquired with the Manager about the facility for sightseeing. He was kind enough to inform all about. He also arranged through one of his staffs two tourist Bus tickets for next day's local sightseeing programme. Meanwhile my wife had already instructed the cook for our breakfast and also instructed him for arranging our lunch.

In the evening we visited the Holy Dwarkadhish (Lord Krishna) Temple. Dwarka is one of the Holiest Hindu cities in the country dedicated to both Lord Vishnu and Lord Shiva. Located in the western coast line of India Dwarka is considered as one of the four Holy Char Dhams. This is dedicated to Lord Vishnu. The other three Vishnu Dhams are the Jagannath Temple at Puri in the Eastern coast line, Ramanathaswamy Temple in Rameshwaram in the Southern coastline and the Badrinath Temple in the Himalaya Mountain in the North. We were lucky to attend the Evening Aarti of the Lord Dwarkadhish. For half an hour we felt as if we were transferred to a different world. After the Aarti we took the blessings of Lord Vishnu and made a complete round of the temple to see the other temples in the complex and spent our evening in Krishna's darshan.

Next morning we reached the Tourism office early. We get into the desired Tourist Bus and occupied the marked seats as per the ticket. Tour guide accompanying us informed that the Bus will take us to seven different tourist spots in a half-day tour. Within half an hour bus started. Our first spot was the Holy Nageshwar Jyotirlinga.

Nageshwar Jyotirlinga is one of the 12 Jyotirlinga shrines mentioned in the Shiva Purana. Nageshwar is believed to be the first such shrine. Bus stopped at a distance and we walked down the approach road to reach the temple. From outside I took a few shots pf the temple.

The location of Jyotirling Shrine is on the route between Dwarka city and Bhet Dwarka Island on the coast of Saurashtra in Gujarat. We entered the temple and walked through a big hall. It leads to the place duly fenced. Through a stare case we walked down to reach underground sanctum sanctorum (Garbhagriha). We were standing before the Swyambhu (self-existent) Jyotirlinga. About 7-8 inch of the Linga top was visible. Rest of the Linga was covered with silver. A snake hood made of silver was protecting the Lord. We stood before the Lord and offered in silence our prayers with reverence in hearts. Then we left the Garbhagriha and climbed up the stare to come back to the hall. Photography was not allowed inside and hence the scanned photos available are shown below.

The Shiva Purana says Nageshwar Jyotirlinga is in 'the Darukavana', which is an ancient name of a forest in India. As per the Shiva Purana there lived a demon named Daruka. His wife Daaruki, a demoness worshipped Mata Parvati. As a result of her penance and devotion, Mata Parvati enabled her to master the forest where she performed her devotions and renamed the forest as 'Darukavana' in her honour. Wherever Daaruki went the forest followed her. In order to save the demons of Darukavana from the punishment of the gods, Daaruka summoned up the power Parvati had given her. She then moved the entire forest into the sea. They continued their campaign against the hermits, kidnapping people and keeping them confined in their new prison under the sea. Among them was a Shiva devotee named Supriya. Demon Daruka attacked and imprisoned him along with many others in his city of Darukavana. This was a city under the sea inhabited by sea snakes and demons. The arrival of Supriya caused a revolution. He set up a lingam and made the prisoners recite the mantra *Om Namaha Shivay* in honour of Shiva. He continued his prayer to the lingam. At the urgent exhortations of Supriya, the prisoners started to chant the holy mantra of Shiva. The demons responded to the chanting by trying to kill Supriya. Immediately they were thwarted when Lord Shiva appeared in his divine form. Shiva handed him a divine weapon (Paasupata Astram) that saved his life. The demon was vanquished and Lord Shiva stayed back there in the form of a Jyotirlinga. Set up by Supriya this Lingam manifestation of Shiva is worshipped as Nageshwar Jyotirlinga.

There was another legend which goes as: 'Balakhilyas', a group of dwarf sages worshipped Lord Shiva in Darukavana for long a time. To test their devotion and patience, Shiva came to them as a nude ascetic wearing only nagas [serpants] on his body. Wives of sages got attracted to the saint and went after him, leaving their husbands behind. Sages got very disturbed and outraged by this. They lost their patience and cursed the ascetic to lose his linga [one of the limited meanings is Phallus, but it has a deeper theistic symbolism]. Shiva linga fell on the earth and the whole world trembled. Lord Brahma and Lord Vishnu came to Lord Shiva, requesting him to save the earth from destruction and take back his linga. Shiva consoled them and took back his linga. Mention of this is available in the Vamana Purana. Lord Shiva promised his divine presence in Darukavana as 'Jyothirlinga' forever and the Jyotirlinga was named as Nageshwar or Nagnath Mahadev. In the Dwadash (12th) Jyotirlinga Stotram Shankaracharya praised this Jyotirlinga as Naganath.

We completed our Darshan of the Jyotirlinga with all humility and reverence. We walked around the shrine with devotion. Coming out to the open premise we found a big old banyan tree situated on the premise. The presence of this banyan tree made the place very pure and pious. We seated under it for a while and thank it for providing us peace of mind.

Nageshwar Mahadev Jyotirlinga Shrine

Then we walked down to the adjacent place where we found a 25 metre tall statue of a sitting Lord Shiva and a large garden with a pond making the place rather very serene. Some archaeological excavations claim five earlier cities at the site.

After leaving the Nageshwar Jyotirlinga the bus took us to the remaining sites which were all mythologically associated with Lord Krishna. For next four hours we felt as if we were in the midst of the Lord Krishna's tenure roaming through sites of Beth Dwarka to Mata Rukmini's temple at the end. At the end of the tour we were dropped at the city market area where we had our lunch and went back to hotel. After taking rest sometimes in the hotel we decided to spend the evening at the Dwarka sea beach. We both sat down on the back of the Dwarkadhish Temple steps.

We saw the waves from the Arabian Ocean were breaking on the temple steps one after the other.

Next day we visited Porbandar town at about 110 km from Dwarka in a day trip. We felt ourselves gratified after our visit to Mahatma Gandhiji's Birth place. That was another Jewel we added to our Travel Crown.

Early next morning we had our return train. We liked Dwarka as a Holy City. It is yet to be spoiled from the tourism point of view. Tourism officials were very co-operating. We had a very satisfying trip. We would never forget our stay at Dwarka.

Chapter Seventeen

Solution Provider Rameshwar Mahadev

That was the fifty ninth spring of my life. We have just settled down in Kolkata.

We were young when we decided that we would visit all the twelve Jyotirlingas in our life time. Age has now started telling upon us slowly. A few more Jyotirlingas are yet to be seen. So were in look out for suitable travel opportunity. Lord Shiva perhaps read our mind.

Next travel opportunity came soon as if it was God sent. We heard about the IRCTC tourism's new tour package launched on the eve of 125th Birth anniversary of Swami Vivekananda. The tour would cover most important places of South India (spanning 11 N and 12 days). The places that would be touched were Hyderabad city, Mysore city, Bangalore city, and Trivandrum city, Kanyakumari, Rameshwaram and Madurai. Visiting all those cities in one go was definitely an attraction which we could not skip.

From Kanyakumari we reached Rameshwaram early in the morning and were transferred to hotel. We got freshened up quickly for Temple darshan. Rameshwaram is an island town in the midst of the Bay of Bengal Sea and connected to the main land through two bridges, known as Pamban bridges. Rameswaram Island is also known as Pamban Island. This island is separated from mainland India by the Pamban channel. This island is about 50 km from Mannar Island of Sri Lanka, the closest point on Sri Lanka. Location of the Manner Island is in the Gulf of Mannar, at the very tip of the Indian peninsula, Rameswaram Island. Rameswaram is the terminus of the railway line from Chennai and Madurai. Like Varanasi, Hindus consider Rameswaram as another most Holy place. It is also one of the Lord Vishnu Char Dham pilgrimages (other three Dhams are Puri in the East, Dwarka in the West and Badrinath in the north).

It is said that a place named Sethu Karai near the sea shore on the sand island of Rameshwaram is associated with Hindu mythology. This is the place where Rama installed a Shiva Linga and prayed to him. Shiva appeared and offered Rama boon to fulfil his wishes and disappeared. It is said Lord Rama then started building a floating bridge on the sea from this place which happened to be closest to the Lanka coast.

Reaching in front of the Shrine we found a long queue of worshippers. Soon we also made room for ourselves in the queue there barefooted. Entering inside the temple we were struck with the awesome architectural beauty and the hugeness of the structure. The temple has four doors all leading to the central temple. We proceeded to visit Shiva Jyotirlingam first and bought ticket for having quick and satisfied Darshan of the Lord Shiva. As advised by the person in the counter we also collected Gangajal from there and proceeded to the central sanctum through the stipulated route.

This large expansive temple is situated on a big island of sand in the Ramnad district of Tamilnadu. The main entrance of the temple tower has many storeys and stands tall. Its structure carvings, statutes and the peaks make people dumb founded. The wilderness of the inside decorated with beautiful stone wall carvings and stone sculptures all along were treating to eyes. The temple is famous in the world for its typical architectural marvel. The grandeur of the Lord is really felt here. The human weakness for being narrow-minded is automatically removed.

We in the queue climbed up the stairs to reach in front of the Garbhagriha. After sometime our turn came to be before the Holy Jyotirlinga God. We handed over our offerings and the Ganga water to the priest and paid our reverence and pray before Lord Shiva. Priest in turn gave back some flowers and Bilva leaves. After that we took a round of the sanctum and exit from the other side of the temple.

Every day, right from 4am till 10pm devotees keep coming to the temple and prayers go on. After the Aarti at night, the Lord is made to sleep in a Golden swing.

Photography inside the temple was not allowed. Above is the scanned copy of the photograph as was available on sale there. Coming out of the temple we took a few more photographs of the outer view of the Great Shrine.

In the Skanda Purana and Shivapurana Rameshwaram is shown as a very important place. The legend of Rameshwar goes like this:

After Sita's abduction by Ravana, Shri Ram wandered in the jungles looking for her. While doing so, he met Sugriva, King of the Monkeys and made friends with him. Rama liked his lieutenant Hanuman and send him as special messenger to find Sita's where about. On his return Rama understood Sita's location in the Lanka. Rama then prepared an army of monkeys to invade Ravana's empire. They reached the southern seashore near Rameswaram. He did not have any means of crossing the sea. Lakshman and Sugriva saw Rama, who is a Shiva devotee in great anguish and could do nothing. Rama was aware that Ravana received some special boons from Lord Shiva and was appeared very worried.

In the mean time, Rama was felt thirsty. Just as he was about to drink water, he remembered that he was yet to perform Shiva pooja. He immediately made a Parthiv Linga and worshipped it with sixteen methods, i.e., Shodasopachar Vidhis. He prayed to Lord Shiva ardently and soulfully. He sang songs of Lord Shiva's praise in a loud voice. He danced and made the sounds of "Aagad bam bam". This pleased Lord Shiva. He instantly appeared before Rama and told him that he could ask for any boons that he would grant them. Ram showed a lot of care, affection and loves to Lord Shiva and prayed and paid obeisance. Rama said "If You want to grant me my wishes, please stay on this earth for the sake of all make it holy". Shiva granted the same by saying "Evamastu" meaning "so be it". He thus stayed there and came to be known as Rameshwara Mahadev in the form of a Shiva Linga and became popular as Rameshwar Jyotirlinga. With the blessings of Lord Shiva, Rama killed all the demons including Ravana and became victorious. Anyone who takes a Darshan of

the Jyotirlinga at Rameshwaram and sprinkles the holy water of the river Ganga attains salvation, Kaivalya Moksha or Nirvana. The Ramanathaswamy Temple thus stand dedicated to Lord Shiva and become famous as Rameswara Mahadev Jyotirlinga. Rameswara means "Lord of Rama" in Sanskrit, an epithet of Shiva, the presiding deity of the Ramanathaswamy Temple. At the same time the temple also become famous as one of the Char-Dhams dedicated to Lord Vishnu. Thus Rameswaram Mahadev Jyotirlinga shrine in the Rameswaram town become a Holy pilgrimage site for both Shaivas and Vaishnavas.

Another version of a legend goes as follows: As per Ramayana, Rama returned to Rameswaram from Lanka after killing Ravana and rescuing his wife Sita. Demon King Ravana was a Brahmana and hence Rama committed a sin. So he decided to pray before Lord Shiva here to absolve the sin. He wanted to build the largest lingam to worship Shiva and directed Hanuman to bring the lingam from Himalayas. Since it took longer to bring the lingam, Sita, meanwhile built a small lingam out of the sand available in the sea shore. This is believed to be the lingam in the sanctum. The primary deity of the temple is Ramanathaswamy in the form of lingam. There is also the other Linga brought by Lord Hanuman from Kailash called Vishwalingam residing simultaneously there. Lord Rama instructed that Vishwalingam should be worshipped first since it was brought by Lord Hanuman - the tradition continues even today.

After our darshan of Lord Rameshwar we engaged ourselves in exploring the entire temple complex. The more we saw more we got wondered on seeing the splendid architectural structure. There is high compound wall on all four sides of the temple premises. It has three striking long corridors in its interior, running between huge colonnades. The Second corridor is formed by sandstone pillars, beams and ceiling. The junction of the third corridor on the west and the paved way coming from the western Gopuram to Setu Madhava (Lord Vishnu) shrine forms a unique structure in the form of a chess board. So it is popularly known as Chokkattan Mandapam.

This Island shrine consists of 24 odd holy water sources viz., Rama Teerth, Sita Kund, Jata Teerth, Lakshman Teerth, etc. The water at all these places is sweet and has a taste of its own. Every Teerth has a typical story attached to it. Devotees take bath with water from all these teerthas before having Darshan of the Jyotirling and feel purged by doing so.

We then visited the temple of Goddess Parvati locally known as Parvathavardhini temple located near by the Rameshwar Mahadev temple. We then looked forward to visit the shrine of Lord Vishnu (locally known as Sethu Madhavar Shrine). We were told earlier that it was located between third and second Corridor. We reached the place after crossing Sethu Madhavar theertham west of the third corridor. The statue of Sethu Madhav is beautifully engraved in the white marble on the west side of the third corridor. The legend associated with this temple is as follows: Long ago there was a king named Sundarapandiyan (alias Punniya Nithi) ruled Madurai region including Rameswaram. One day he came to Sethu (Old name of Rameswaram) with his wife Vindhavani and his army. He conducted a Special yagna dedicated to Vishnu for the welfare of his family and country. After being pleased by the Yagna Vishnu sent his wife in the form of orphan girl. Seeing the lonely little girl in the temple he asked her who was she and why was she alone. Girl replied to king that she was an orphan. The Pandyan king lovingly adopted her as his daughter. King named her as Guna Nithi and brought her up under his protection.

After few days a black Brahmin man wearing Rudraksa garland holding Gangajal container on shoulder and palm leaf fan in hands. Guna Nithi was then picking flower in the garden. The Brahmin suddenly forcibly held the hand of the girl. Immediately the servants of the king took that man to the king and complained about him. The king ordered his men to enchain and imprison him in the temple itself. That man was chained in the place where Sethu Madhav temple is now.

At the same night Lord Vishnu appeared in the dream the King had. He showed himself as the chained Brahmin and King's adopted daughter as her consort. He suddenly woke up and went to the place where that Brahmin was enchained. He saw Lord Vishnu there and her adopted daughter adorned with jewels as a Lakshmi, the consort of Vishnu. The King was ashamed for his conduct and prayed mercy for his mistake. Lord Vishnu was pleased. He assured the King that he would stay in this temple chained along with Lakshmi and bless the devotees under the name Sethu Madhavar. Since then Lord Vishnu is being worshipped there in the temple as Sethu Madhavar. Besides this, there are temples of Sanatan Ganapati, Veerabhadra Hanuman, Navagraha, etc, which we visited.

As the history goes Rameswaram used to be a transit point to reach Sri Lanka (old name Ceylon) primarily to receive the blessings of Lord Ramanathaswamy. The 7th and 8th century Tamil compositions were the major source of information about the temple. After having a short control over the town by Chola king Rajendra Chola I (1012 – 1040 CE) the Jaffna kingdom (1215– 1624 CE) grabbed the island and claimed to be custodians of the Rameswaram.

Afterwards Rameshwaram was captured by Alauddin Khilji, the ruler of Delhi Sultanate in early 14th century. Later during the early 15th century, the place came under the Pandya dynasty. Then in 1520 CE, the town came under the rule of Vijayanagara Empire. The Sethupathis, the breakaway from Madurai Nayaks, ruled Ramanathapuram and renovated the Ramanathaswamy temple. The region was repeatedly captured by outsiders in the 18th century. By the end of 18th century Rameswaram came under the British East India Company. It was annexed to the Madras Presidency. After 1947, the town became a part of Independent India.

Our visit to Rameshwar Mahadev Jyotirlinga was a great experience as we were just lost amidst the vast ocean of mythology prevailed there. We offered our obedience and reverence to both Lord Shiva and Lord Vishnu in a very divine ambience.

Chapter Eighteen

Miraculous Kind Tryambakeshwar

That was October, sometime after the Durga Puja.

My son was then settled at his new place of job. It was his wish to take us on a holiday excursion.

I took this opportunity to make the trip a mixed one combining pilgrimage with relaxation. Accordingly we decided to visit Nasik and Aurangabad. Selecting Nasik had two-fold purpose – it was the place, where Tryambakeshwar Mahadev Temple, one of the twelve Jyotirlingas was located. Triyambak, the place as known is also the place from where the river Godavari is said to have originated.

We reached Nasik Road station by Geetanjali Exp where our son joined us. Together we checked in to our reserved Hotel at Nasik. It was a nice 3-star hotel situated in the heart of the town.

Next morning we arranged a local cab for sightseeing. The first site we visited was the Tryambakeshwar Mahadev temple. The temple is one of the holiest and sacred places for Hindu pilgrims and is revered as one of the 12 Jyotirlingas Shrines of Lord Shiva. The temple lies in the foothill of mountain Brahmagiri which is origin of the Holy River Godavari. It is known locally as river Gautami. The great temple is standing on the bank of the river Gautami.

There was a sacred pond called "Kushavarta". It is said to be customary to take a dip there before visiting the Jyotirlinga. So after getting down from our car we walked down the temple premise to reach the sacred tank Kushavarta. That was about a few minutes' walk from the main temple. It is believed that the pond is caused by the accumulation of water of the river Godavari sipped through a hidden passage immediately after emerging from the Brahmagiri hills. From here the river hide in the earth-bed before exiting to take her route to the rest of its passage through Nasik city. People believe a dip in this sacred river wipes off the sins.

We stood knee-dip in the Holy pond for a while with all reverence and then took holy water on both palm and sprinkled on us.

Kushavarta Teertha

The legend about the Kushavarta has that Sage Gautam by mistake killed a cow once and earned a sin. To get rid of his sin he was required to bath in the holy river Ganga. Through a great penance he satisfied Lord Shiva and brought down Ganga in the name of River Godavari. But River Godavari as being the Ganga River was not willing to leave Lord Shiva and played hide and seek with Sage Gautama. Gautama with deep meditation and Tapasya forced the river Godavari to stall within the enchanted grass area he made around and put a vow on her. He did this and took a holy bath in this water and got rid of his sin for killing a cow. The pond is a Holy Teertha to all Hindus since then.

From here we walk down to the main temple. As usual cameras & mobiles were not allowed. Entry to the temple was to be made on bare foot only. We bought tickets to enter into the temple for a comfortable Darshan. My wife bought flowers and bilva leaves for offerings to Lord Shiva. We walked pass the Nandi temple first situated outside the main temple premises. We entered the temple arena which was a huge area. Through the zigzag fencing we reached in front of the temple door. We found the place of the Jyotirlinga, about 5 meters away from the Garbhagriha entrance Gate where we were standing. The level of Jyotirlinga was seen at a lower level 3 ft below the Garbhagriha floor. One has to go down through steps from the door and reach there if he is to touch the linga or do Abhishek. But we were to pay our darshan from above.

We found this great Swyambhu Jyotirlinga has a very uniquely evolved form. With much surprise we noticed that no Linga shaft seen protruded vertically upward. There was just the bottom part of the pounding stone (Ukhali), instead. There was seen a circular shape cut in that stone forming a deep hole. Inside the hole we found there were three pindies shaped like the thumb.

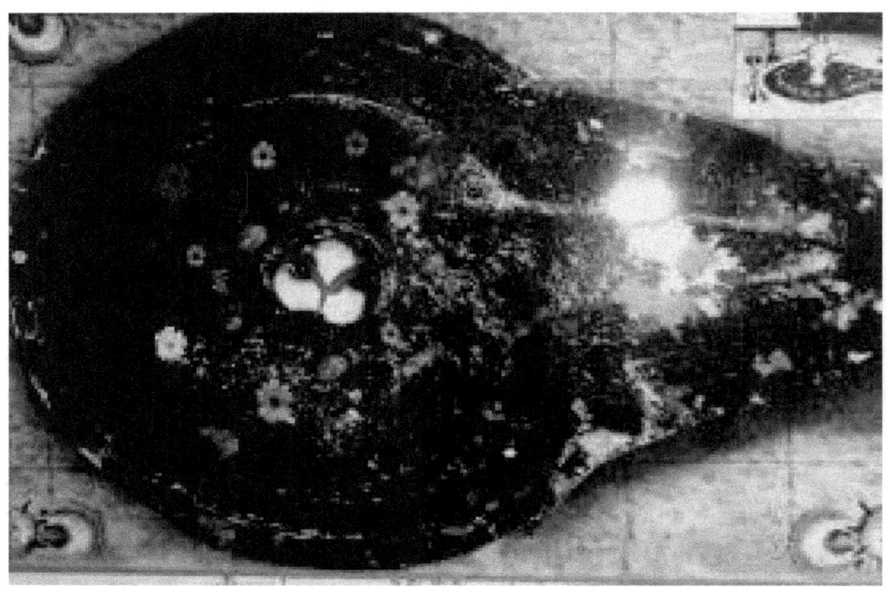

They represent the forms of the three deities, Brahma, Vishnu and Maheshwara symbolically. Surprisingly on the Pindi of Maheswara water drops were seen continuously sipping through an orifice in the stone. Nobody knows from where the water comes and does natural Abhishekam on Lord Shiva's pindi. This is considered as a miracle. These three uniqueness viz. the shape, presence of trinities and auto abhishekam, made this Jyotirling linga most distinctive among the twelve Jyotirlingas. Presence of Trinities further made this Jyotirlinga known as Tryambakeshwar Jyotirlinga and is extremely reverend to Hindus.

With due reverence and respect we offered our prayer before the Jyotirlinga and took the blessings from the Pujariji. After the darshan from the distance, we were told to have another peaceful reflective darshan of the Lord in the mirror attached by sitting in the middle of the dome inside the temple. After this darshan through the mirror reflection of this great linga just for a few seconds I felt a great power and sense of bliss and blessings from the Lord. Then we walked around the shrine before coming out of the temple. As photography was not allowed inside the temple two scanned copy of the photographs of the Jyotirlinga as available there are reproduced below.

Legend associated with this great shrine of Lord Shiva has it:

Many centuries ago, this place was full of Rishis and Sadhus. They used to meditate here and hence this land was called a tapobhoomi. Gautam Rishi (one of the Saptarishis) used to stay here with his wife Ahilya. Once this place was without rain for several years and faced severe drought. The land was drying up and life forms were disappearing. Seeing these conditions of drought the residents, the saints and all the birds and animals started fleeing from there. Worried Sage Gautam then engaged himself in the Tapasya on the Dakshina Mountain. He did great Mangalik tapasya through Pranayama for six long months with great penance. Varuna, the Deva of rains, was pleased and appeared before Gautama, who in turn asked for water. At the behest of Varuna, Gautam dug a hole on his land. With the help of Varuna's miraculous power, it filled with water. Varuna said, "Due to the power of your penance, this hole would be an unending source of water "Akshya". It will become famous by your name. It will augment all holy rituals like Yagna, Dana, Tapa, Homa Shradha, and worship of Gods". Acquiring water the saints started making preparations for the Yagna and the production of "Breehika". Thus Gautam Rishi by using his power of meditation created a small pond of water for only meeting their urgent needs. The conditional use of water as directed by the Rishi Gautam was not liked by other Rishis and their wives. They became jealous of power of meditation of Gautam Rishi. They decided to get rid of Gautam's fame and ego. So all these Rishis performed Yagna and invoked Lord Ganesha. Rishis asked Lord Ganesh to become a cow and die at Gautam's hermitage so that he may incur the sin of killing a cow "Gohatya".

Hearing this unscrupulous plan Lord Ganesha was unhappy. He warned the Rishis that this was a misdeed and it would not do any favour. But Rishis were adamant on this one wish. Finally granting them the wish as a fruit of the Yagna, Lord Ganesha went in Gautam's hermit in the form of a weak and feeble cow. When Gautam Rishi went to feed that cow she died. Some Rishis saw this and grabbed the opportunity and accused Gautama of slaying a cow "Gohatya". They insulted Gautama Rishi and his wife Ahilya by saying that they have acquired a sin by killing a cow. Hence they have to undertake a Holy deep in the sacred Ganga River to wash their sin. Those Sages might have thought that it would be quite difficult for Rishi Gautam to achieve that feat.

Gautama Rishi along with wife Ahilya did great penance and started meditating on Lord Shiva. Many years passed meditating. By his severe penance Lord Shiva became pleased and appeared along with Brahma, Vishnu, Ganesha, three Goddesses and all the Gods at this place to grant him a boon. Lord Shiva told him that he was indeed a pure soul and a great Mahatma. A great injustice was done to him. Shiva told him that he could ask for some boons. Gautam Rishi asked for River Ganga from Lord Shiva and asked him to stay at this place forever to benefit of mankind. Lord Shiva hitted his hair lock (Jataa) on the Brahmagiri Mountain and from there river Ganga sprang up and came down in the name of Gautami or Godavari. Lord Shiva along with Lord Vishnu and Lord Brahma remained here in the form of Linga.

Feeling blessed we came out of the main shrine. We viewed the temple from outside. The courtyard was very huge open space. The temple was made up of black stones with lot of small Shivalingas in the small temples near the walls. The boundary is also covered with huge fort like wall to protect it from the attacks from the outside invaders. It is said that there used to be two kalashes in the temple full of Gold. This temple was completed in 16th century and it is said that the cost incurred to build the temple at that time was Rs.16 lakhs.

After coming out of the temple premise we collected our mobiles, cameras, etc. We then took several pictures of the temple from outside. Later on after having a quick breakfast we ventured into covering other important holy places in the Tryambak town. Each of these holy places had its mythological background. We saw the adjacent Brahmagiri Mountain and stood before a long steps going up in the mountain. After taking complete information from the local people we started for the Gangadwar, the birth place of river Godavari. We covered the 700 steps to reach the mountain. From there through a long walk, sometimes through narrow passage and sometimes plain land on mountain top we reached the desired place.

Tryambakeshwar temple from outside

The spring at Brahmagiri from where Godavari comes out, is known as Gangadwar. The Ganga water flows from a rock shaped like a cow face, constantly. The temple of Godavari Mata is located here. Soon we started our downward return journey to the Nashik city.

After emanating from Gangadwar, the river Godavari thins down and almost disappears, only to appear again at Tahalhati down below in the Nashik city. In order to prevent it from disappearing, Gautam Rishi threw Darbhas on all four sides. Because of this, Godavari flows in Kushavarta. It is built very strong. There are steps on all four sides to facilitate going down to the waters. At the time of Simhasta (in Leo), every 12 years, a Kumbh mela is held here. Lakhs of people take a holy dip in Kushavarta. On all the four sides of Kushavarta corridors are built.

Beautiful statues are also carved here in the Brahmagiri Talhati, near Kushavarta, there is a big lake called Ganga Sagar.

On the Parikrama path, there are beautiful places like Ram Teerth. Prayag Teerth and Nrisimha Teerth etc, The Peshwa kings planted trees at every 25 hand distance. During the reign of the Peshwas, criminals were asked to do the Parikrama (circumbulation) of Brahmagiri as punishment.

The Tryambakeshwar JyotirLinga is unique. Holy Tryambak town is a wonderful place of pilgrimage. Our trip is still lingering in our heart and soul, always provoking us to rush there once again.

Chapter Nineteen

Kind Leveller Grishneshwar

After paying our respects to Tryambakeshwar Mahadev, we left Nasik next afternoon for Aurangabad.

Aurangabad is just 3 hrs rail journey from Nasik. We reached Aurangabad in the late evening and straightway checked into our reserved hotel. The hotel was situated in the heart of the city. We completed a nice dinner with Chinese preparation in the rooftop hotel restaurant itself.

Next day we arranged a car with the help of the hotel for sightseeing. We started a little early in the morning to visit Lord Shani temple at Shani Shinganapur which was 65 km from Aurangabad and located in the Ahmadnagar district in Maharashtra. After offering our reverence and pray to Lord Shani we came back to Aurangabad and then proceeded to Devagiri (Daulatabad).

We reached a place called Verul, which lies at a distance of 11 km from Daulatabad (Devagiri) and 30 km from Aurangabad city. It lies at a close proximity to the Ellora caves. Here located the Grishneshwar Mahadev temple, which is one of the twelfth Jyotirlinga shrines mentioned in the Shiva Purana (Kotirudra Samhita, Ch.32-33 referred as "Grishneshwar Jyotirlinga"). This is believed to be the last or 12th Jyotirlinga on the earth.

Verul was originally a settlement of the Naga tribes. Naga settlement was known as Bambi, which in Marathi known as "Varul". "Varul" gradually changed into "Verul" and the place become known by this name only. The River Yelaganga flows here. The name "Verul" is derived from Yelaganga, on whose banks the village is located. There was a king by the name "Yela" here. The capital of his kingdom was Yelapar, or Yelur or Verul.

Driver parked our car at the stipulated parking place. We walked up the steps to enter the temple premise. Before entering the premises we took a few shots of the surroundings. The open temple premise was huge. We stood at a distance to take a view of the gigantic temple. The temple was built of red rocks and was composed of a five tier Shikara. It is believed that one very devoted Shiva devotee Bhonsle (The Chief of Verul) once found a treasure hidden in the snake pit (ant hill) by the grace of Lord Grishneshwar. He spent that money to renovate the temple and built a lake in Shikharshinganapur. Later it was restored in the 18th century by Rani Ahilyabai Holker. The temple is 240 x 185 feet tall. It housed beautiful carvings and sculptures of many Indian Gods and Goddesses (Dash avatars are depicted in the carving). These were beautiful to look at particularly because of the red stones used. There were also other beautiful statutes carved out. A court hall was built on 24 pillars. On these pillars there were wonderful carvings. The scenes and paintings were beautiful. The Grabhagriha was said to measure 17ft x 17 ft. The Lingamurthy faces eastward. There was a gorgeous Nandi seating on the centre of the court hall.

According to Sthala Purana the legend of the place goes like this;

King of the place was engaged in hunting once. While hunting, he killed the animals living with the Rishis and Munis too. Seeing this, the irate Saints cursed the king, as a result of which, his entire body was infested with insects. Smitten by this curse, the king began to wander in the forest. His throat was parched because he was very thirsty. No water was available nearby. Suddenly he found a water hole made by the hooves of a horse. Just as the king started to drink water a miracle occurred. The King's body was rid of all the insects. Grateful King did severe penance (Tapa) there. Lord Brahma was pleased and appeared before him and installed Parashta Teerth there. He also created a huge and holy lake nearby. This Brahma Sarovar later came to be known as Shivalay. Following separate legend was also available about Shivalay;

Lord Shiva and his wife Parvati were playing chess on Mount Kailash. Goddess Parvati checkmated Shiva. Disappointed with the defeat Shiva went away southward. He went and stayed at a place on the Sahyadri range which had cool breeze blowing all the time. This place was given the name of Maheshamauli or Bhainsmal. Parvati came there looking for Shankar. She won the heart of Shiva in the form of a hill mountain tribal girl. They both spent some time there happily. The forest came to be known as Kamyakavana. Lord Mahesha forbade crows from entering the area of Maheshamauli or Bhainsmal. One day, Parvati was very thirsty. Shankara pierced earth with his trident and got the water of Bhogavati from the Patal (Nether world). This was one set of legend behind the Shivalay.

One set of legend behind the creation of Grishneshwar Mahadev Jyotirlinga goes like this - The Shivalay expanded a little ahead to meet Shivanadi and a little further river Yelaganga was flowing by. When Shiva and Parvati were staying here happily, a hunter by the name Sudhanwa came there looking for a prey. A miracle happened and Sudhanwa turned into a woman. At this he did a severe Tapa there. Lord Shiva was pleased and appeared. Actually, Sudhanwa was a woman by birth in his previous life. Shiva turned Sudhanwa into Yelaganga River. Thus, Punya Sarita Yelaganga was born in the Kamyavan. Later, it was to become the bathing place called Dhara Teerth or 'Sita's Snangriha' and flow from a higher place and goes through Verul village.

Once Parvati, was about to fill her hair parting with vermillion and saffron, in Kamyavan. She kept them in her left palm and mixed the water of Shivalay in it. With the right thumb she started mixing them both. Then a miracle occurred, vermillion turned into a Shivalinga and a great light appeared in it. Parvati was awe struck at this. Then Lord Shiva said: "This Linga was hidden in the Patala" and removed it with his trident. Then a bubble emerged from the earth with water (Kashikhand). Parvati kept that glorious light in stone Linga and installed it there. This Purna (complete) JyotirLinga is called Kunkumeshwar. But Dakshayani created this Linga with the function of her thumb. She gave it the name of Grishneshwar Mahadev (Grishna means friction).

Grishneshwar Mahadev is also known as Ghushmeshwar Mahadev and the most popular legend behind goes as follows; According to Shivapurana, in the southern direction, on a mountain named Devagiri lived a great scholar Brahmin Sudharm of Bharadwaj gotra along with his wife Sudeha. The couple did not have a child because of which Sudeha was very unhappy and sad. Sudeha prayed and tried all possible remedies but in vain. They were harassed and tortured by the sly remarks of their neighbours. But Sudhama, an intelligent person, did not care about these. Frustrated of being childless, Sudeha got her sister Ghushma married to her husband. Both of them promised that there would be no jealousy between them. On the advice of her sister, Ghushma used to make 101 lingas, worship them and discharge them in the nearby lake. With the blessings of Lord Shiva, Ghushma gave birth to a boy. After sometime Ghushma got her son married. Both Sudharm and Dushma were nice to Sudeha. But jealousy did get the better of Sudeha. Out of jealousy, one night she killed Ghushma's son and threw him in the lake where Ghushma used to discharge the lingas.

Next morning, Ghushma and Sudharm got involved in daily prayers and ablutions. Sudeha too, got up and started performing her daily choirs. Ghushma's daughter-in-law, however, saw stains of blood on her husband's bed and parts of the body drenched in blood. Being horrified, she narrated everything to mother-in-law Ghushma who was absorbed in worshipping Shiva. Ghushma did not deter. Even her husband Sudharm did not move an inch. Even when Ghushma saw the bed drenched in blood she did not break down and said he who has given me this child shall protect him and started reciting 'Shiva-Shiva'. Later, when she went to discharge the Shivalingas after prayers she saw her son coming. Seeing her son Ghushma was neither happy nor sad. At that time Lord Shiv appeared before her and said he was pleased with her devotion and informed that her own sister had killed her son. But Ghushma told Lord Shiva to forgive Sudeha and emancipate her. Pleased with her generosity, Lord Shiva asked her another boon. Ghushma said that if he was really happy with her devotion then he should reside here eternally for the benefit of the mankind in the form of a Jyotirling which may be known by her name. On her request, Lord Shiva manifested himself in the form of a Jyotirlinga and assumed the name Ghushmeshwar. The lake was named as Shivalaya thereafter. We were told that Holy water was springing from inside the temple.

We enter the main temple and stood before the Nandi, the vehicle of Lord Shiva for a while. We male worshipers were asked to take out the dress and bare the upper part of the body. Ladies were asked to fully cover their heads with sari or dopatta, etc. before entering the sanctum sanctorum. We could touch the

Jyotirlinga with the permission of the Pujariji and offered our reverence and pray to Lord Shiva and also to Goddess Parvati.

This was done as Goddess Parvati was also worshipped their along with Lord Shiva. As cameras and mobiles were not allowed, so scanned copies of the available photographs of the Grabhagriha are shown here. We stood inside the temple for a while. The sacred and peaceful ambience took us to Gods world. The interesting thing to us was that Goddess Parvati was also worshipped here with equal reverence and somber.

Both Goddess Parvati & Lord Shiva being worshipped

After sometimes we came out of the temple and moved around the open courtyard and saw the surroundings. Finally before coming out we collected back our mobiles and cameras. We then took some photographs from outside the temple boundary.

The Grishneshwar Jyotirlinga Temple is one of the ancient and holiest shrines of India. The temple stands as an illustration of the pre-historic temple traditions as well as of the pre-historic architectural style and structure. The inscriptions on the temples are a source of much attraction to ardent travellers. The temple reflects of south Indian temple architectural style and structure. The temple is built of red rocks in the form of a five-tier Shikara. The temple structure was destroyed by the Delhi Sultanate in 13th and 14th-century. The temple went through several rounds of rebuilding followed by re-destruction during the Mughal-Maratha conflict. The temple was re-constructed by grandfather of Shivaji Maloji Bhosale of Verul in the 16th century. It was rebuilt in the current form in the 18th century under the sponsorship of Queen Ahilyabai Holker of Indore, after the fall of the Mughal Empire.

We returned with a happy memory of our Darshan of Lord Grishneshwar Mahadev. On the way back to city we visited a few more historical places of Aurangabad as well and filled our memory bag.

Chapter Twenty

Great Rescuer of Mankind Bhimashankar

That was end Oct 2016. My son had earlier proposed to take us to visit one of the 12th Jyotirlinga Bhimashankar Mahadev Jyotirlinga.

Bhimashankar Mahadev Temple is situated in the Bhimashankar Mountain in the Sahyadri Range on the Western Ghat mountain chain. Two other mountain peaks located there named Bhavargiri and Rathachal. The place is located ahead of Ghodegaon in the Rajgurunagar (Khed) tehsil in Pune district at a distance of 125 km.

We reached Pune from Kolkata and son joined us there. We hired a cab from Pune and started our journey for Bhimashankar. The route we followed was via Manchar. We passed by Manchar after almost two hours. As we left Manchar behind distant mountain ranges started appearing in our views. They become larger gradually as we crossed Rajgurunagar. Shortly after we were in the midst of hills surrounded from all sides. The place we crossed was Ghodegaon. Finally we entered the valley of Bhimashankar mountain range. After sometimes we reached the place named as Mhatarbachi wadi and found our Resort.

This was the only resort in Bhimashankar. It is situated in the slope of uneven plane of the valley amidst wild grass and forest. The night we spent was one of the scariest nights we had during our travel trip. In the night we were told that a leopard was seen in the surrounding. The resort manager provided us additional security measures. However the night went off without any incidence.

Next morning we were to visit the Jyotirlinga. Resort Manager himself dropped us at the Bhimashankar temple complex. The road route from the resort to the temple place was through the Reserved Forest of the Bhimashankar Wildlife Sanctuary. Our passage through it was mind freshening. It seems as if the Lord Shiva is keeping a silent vigil over the majestic ranges of the Sahyadri. The serenity gets interrupted only by the silent murmuring of the cool breeze and the occasional chirping of birds. We walked down the lane and reached the Bhimashankar temple complex. The temple is located on the banks of the River Chandrabhaga (or Bhima) on the expansive meadows, surrounded by high mountains from all three sides.

The Kund source of River Bhima

River Bhima is said to have originated from the Bhimashankar Mountain. A large number of waterfalls and streams have emerged and flown along the mountain slopes. These streams are believed to have combined into a Kund which we saw and took photograph. In the mythological terms these streams were imagined as the perspiration of Lord Shankar. The Kund is said to be the source of the Bhima River.

We came down from the mountain along the slope to reach the entry Gate of the complex. From there we walked down the wide stairs and reach the Shrine entry point.

We walked down the steps for sometimes and then reached the temple premise. My wife bought flowers and Bilva leaves and other Puja offerings. Moving through the fenced path we reached the Garbhagriha finally. We noticed the silver capped Shivalinga. We could touch the Shivalinga with the help of the Priest. We offered our flowers and leaves along with prayer to Lord directly.

This was an important moment for all of us as earlier we were not allowed to touch the God in other Jyotirlinga temple we visited. All of us felt something inside our soul as soon as we touched the Lingam. This feeling does come from our own faith and belief. We felt the divine feeling within us. The overhead Mirror reflects the Jyotirlinga which can be seen by the devotees from distance who could not enter into the Garvgriha yet.

We understood that the worship of Lord Bhimashankar was done with Rudrabhishek, Panchamrit snan (bathing) everyday. The Lord is praised in rich words. On Mondays as well as other days, lot of devotees flock here for Darshan. Due to restriction we could not take any picture of the Garvgriha. We came out of the Garvgriha and moved around the temple premises.

The legend about Bhimashankar Mahadev goes like this. According to Hindu Purana there lived demons in the Sahyadri Mountains in the ancient times. Their chief by the name Tripurasura become drunk with power. Demons harassed every resident of three worlds - Swarg (Heavens), Narak (Hell) and Patal (Nether world). The divines were very scared. All the Gods and Goddesses approached Lord Shiva for help. Mahadev himself came to destroy Tripurasura. Lord Shankar assumed colossal proportions. Tripurasura feared when they saw this Rudravatar. The fight went on for long. In the end, Lord Shiva killed the wicked demon and set the three worlds (Tribhuvan), free. Lord Shankar in the form of a huge hunk was very tired. In order to get some rest, He settled here on the high area of the Sahyadri mountains. Sweat started pouring down from His huge body in thousands of streams. It all joined together and collected in a pond or Kund. The river that started from there is known as Bhima, which can be seen even today. Devotees prayed to Bhimakaya

Rudra to reside with them forever. Lord Shiva listened to the devotees and agreed to stay there as a Jyotirlinga forever.

According to another legend many years ago in the dense forest of Dakini on the lofty ranges of the Sahyadris lived the evil Asuras led by one named Bhima with his mother Karkati. Demon Bhima was harassing and torturing common men and women. Compassion and kindness shivered in the presence of Bhima. He was hell bent in the path of destruction of Dharma. Whenever he is alone he is often confronted by certain questions about his own existence. This kept tormenting him.

When Bhima could no longer withstand his agony and curiosity, he asked his mother Karkati to unveil the mysteries of his life. He urged his mother to tell about his father. He also wanted to know why he had abandoned them. After much hesitation and with a lingering fear his mother revealed to him that he was the son of the mighty Kumbhakarna, the younger brother of the Lankadheeswara, Ravana. Lord Vishnu in his incarnation as Lord Rama annihilated Kumbhakarna. Karkati told Bhima that her husband and his father were killed by Rama in the Great War. This infuriated Bhima. His mother continued to narrate that she had never seen Lanka. She met Kumbhakarna there at some place at Sahyadri Mountains. After Bhima's birth they continued to stay there. After the death of her husband only her parental place became a refuge of sorts for Bhima. Her parents were Pushkasi and Karkati. When her parents went to eat up Agastya, the saint, he burned them to ashes with the power of his meditation and Tapas. Hearing the story Bhima was raged with anger and he vowed to avenge Lord Vishnu and against all the divines.

To achieve this he embarked on a severe penance or Tapas to please Lord Brahma. The compassionate creator Brahma was pleased by the dedicated devotee and granted him immense prowess. This was a terrible mistake Brahma did. The evil tyrant caused havoc in the three worlds. He defeated King of Gods Indra and conquered the Heavens. He captured all the divines including Lord Vishnu. They were in his control. He also defeated a staunch devotee of Lord Shiva, Kamasarupeshwar and put him in the dungeons. He started torturing Rishis and Sadhus. All these angered the Gods. They along with Lord Brahma begged to Lord Shiva to come for their rescue. Lord Shiva consoles the Gods and agreed to rescue them from the tyrant.

On the other side Bhima started torturing Kamarupeshwar inside the prison. But the King did not stop his worship of Shiva. He performed the Puja with the same devotion, observing all the procedures and his wife also joined him in this. Meanwhile Bhima learnt from someone that Kamarupeshwar was preparing to kill him. On hearing about this, he went straight to the prison and started inquiring into the process and aim of his worship. When he learnt the truth from the king, the wicked Demon called Lord Shiva by name and insulted Him. He insisted and ordered Kamasarupeshwar to worship him instead of Lord Shiva. When Kamarupeshwar denied doing that and refused to do his pooja, tyrant Bhima raised his sword to strike the Shiva Linga to which Kamasarupeshwar was doing abhishekam and pooja, Lord Shiva appeared before him in all his magnificence. A severe fight ensued in which bows, arrows, swords, axe, the disc and trident etc. were used. In the end, at the request of Holy sage Narada to put an end to that war, Lord Shankar blew a fire and burned the wicked Demon Bhima to ashes and concluded the saga of tyranny.

All the Devas were released from their sorrows. All the Gods and the holy sages who were present there together pleaded with Lord Shankar to make this place his abode. Lord Shiva manifested himself in the form of the Bhimashankar Jyotirlingam. It is believed that the sweat that poured forth from Lord Shiva's body after the battle formed the Bhima River. The mountain which is seen in the shape of a chariot becomes the abode of Bhimashankar and the mountain become known as Rathachal.

About self emanating Mahadev the story goes like this: Once there lived a woodcutter named Bhatirao Lakadhara. One day while cutting tree with his axe he found blood oozing out from the earth. He got scared and ran away. Soon a crowd gathered there. Someone brought a milk cow and made it stand there. The milk that came from the cow's udders stopped the bleeding of the earth. Surprising everyone, a glowing Jyotirlinga of Shiva emanated from the earth. People built a temple there and installed the Jyotirlinga in the temple. This temple which is at a height of 1034 mts eventually came to be known as Bhimashankar temple.

After paying our reverence to Lord Shiva we came out from the Jyotirling shrine. First temple we visited in the complex was that of Lord Shani. We offered our prayer there with reverence. Next we took several pictures of the Shrine from the outside.

Glories of Bhimashankar have been aptly described by Gangadhar Pandit, Ramdas, Sridhar Swamy, Narahari Malo, Saint Gnaneshwar, and other saints who described Bhimashankar as Jyotirlinga. Historical figures like Chatrapati Shivaji and Rajaram Maharaj were known to visit this shrine. This was a favourite place for Peshwa Balaji Vishwanath and Raghunath. Peshwa Raghunath had constructed a well there. Diwan of the Peshwa Nana Phadanvis renovated this temple to the present form.

Bhimashankar temple was built in Hemadpanthi style. It was decorated with the Dashavatar statues. These were looking beautiful. The Nandi temple was close to the main temple. A huge bell (unique in Roman style) was located close to the temple. It had 1721 AD inscribed on it and was presented by Chimaji Appa (brother of Bajirao Peshwa I and Uncle Nanasheb Peshwa). We are told when this bell rings, the entire premises reverberate with its echoes.

The natural surrounding amidst which Lord Bhimashankar resided was wonderful. Our mind got cooled and pacified instantly as we roamed around. There are many mythological places in the complex and at the surrounding. Among these which we could visit were Mokshakund, Gyankund, Papanasini, Shri Ram temple, Sakshi Vinayaka, Gorakhnath Ashram, Daityasamharini Kamalaja Devi's place, Kamalaja Lake and Hanuman Lake.

Around the Jyotirlinga temple there were a few natural spots which often attracted tourists. However we could visit the Mumbai Point and the Hanuman Mandir and took many photographs. Mumbai point signifies that if one start walking in a straight line from that point we will reach Mumbai city. We did not visit the third place Nagphoni as that was on the top of the Hill. The entire area was covered with deep forest which was the part of the Bhimashankar Wildlife Sanctuary. Bhimashankar is famous for the Giant Squirrel locally called as "Shekaru" which can be found in the deep forest. We however could not see any Shekaru but only located two of their habitats on the top of the tall tree in the dense forest.

On our way back we could see the Bhima River flowing through at some distance from Bhimashankar. Lord Bhimashankar Mahadev is said to have incarnated as the Savior of not only the mankind but of the entire three worlds. This was said to be the Form of the Almighty where he has been imagined to have engaged in violent war with the Demon and liberated the rest of the mankind. Thus Lord Bhimashankar here is the expression of Strength, Courage and sense of Responsibility. Lord Shiva took himself to an enormous Form to fight the most powerful Demon. The Gigantic proportion of His Form has lead mankind to imagine his presence in the Chariot Form of the mountain, known as The Rathachal Mountain. It has made these picturesque surrounding mythological and generates interests in the human being. People have perceived about Lord Shiva through this wonderful self-emancipated Jyotirlinga.

We were overwhelmed with the vibes of the place and vowed our heads before Lord Shiva. The place is still inconvenient to reach because of the inadequate infrastructure there. We however have liked the place and have carried with us unforgettable experiences. While climbing up the staircase we found many shops were selling special sweets. We could not resist from tasting it. We liked the sweet and bought some for carrying to home.

Chapter Twenty One

Universally Kind Lord Mallikarjuna Mahadev

My son went back to his place of work after Puja holidays. Due to paucity of leave he could not join us when we visited Srisailam in December.

Srisailam, a tribal town is situated on the flat top of the Nallamala hills at an average elevation of 1345 ft, on the southern bank of River Krishna in Kurnool district of Andhra Pradesh. Shri Mallikarjuna Mahadev Temple one of the twelve Jyotirlingas is situated in Srisailam. Srisailam, initially known as Mantharaparvata, is also called by the name Sriparvata or Srigiri. There is a saying in Sanskrit about Srisailam:

"श्रीशैल शिखर दृष्ट्वा पुन: जन्म न विद्यते ।"

"Srisaila Sikhara drstva punah janma na vidyate ।"

Meaning "By seeing the *Sikhara* or the peak of Srisailam, (one releases himself from the cycle of birth and death) one is not born again." Let me tell you a legend about Srisailam.

Once Devas including Lord Kartikeya and Lord Ganesha were in arguments about who would be worshiped first among them, Lord Shiva decided to have a competition. He bade that the one who would complete going round the world in Pradakshinam first would be the "Pratham Pujyate". He opened the competition among all the Devas. All the participating Gods started their race. By the time Lord Kartikeya could go round the world on his Vahana, Lord Ganesha went round his parents 7 times (for according to Shastras, going in Pradakshinam round one's parents is equivalent to going once round the world (Bhupradakshinam). Lord Shiva appreciated Lord Ganesha's intellect and declared that he would be worshiped first in all Pujas henceforth. Kartikeya on his return was enraged and went away to stay alone on Mount Kravunja in the name of Kumarabrahmachari. Lord Shiva decided to see his aggrieved son. On seeing his father coming over to pacify him, he tried to move to another place, but on the request of the Devas, stayed close by. The place where Lord Shiva and Parvati stayed came to be known as Srisailam. Lord Shiva visits Lord Kartikeya on Amavasya day & Parvati Devi on Poornima.

We started our journey from Howrah by train SSPN Express and got down at Markapur Road in AP. We traveled by Bus to cover the distance of 81 km between Srisailam and Markapur town. The hilly track of about 46 km of this distance was through Nallamala Forest full of Kadali and Bilva trees, covering both sides of the road. We travelled through this difficult and partly untouched tribal terrain for almost 3 hrs. Finally we reached Srisailam in the evening and checked in AP Tourism Resort. The resort was good. We took hot water bath which removed our day long exhaustion and refreshened completely. In the night we went out for dinner. We walked down the lane amidst calmness and freshness. Soon we found the Jyotirlinga Shrine of Mallikarjuna Mahadev temple situated very close to our hotel. From there we walked down to reach the market place and found a few restaurants there. We had our dinner in one of the restaurants and return to hotel by 9:30 pm.

Next morning we woke up early and visited the Temple of Lord Mallikarjuna Mahadev. The existing main temple is a huge complex consisting of separate temples of Lord Mallikarjuna

Mahadev and Devi Bhramaramba, several Sub Shrines, Pillared Halls, Mandapas, Springs etc.

The entire complex is fortified by the most impressive Prakaram wall of massive stones. Wall contains hand drawn pictures with no two pictures are identical. That interesting fact motivated us to take a few photographs. The Prakaram wall contains four principal gates at four cardinals surmounted by the Gopuras. The eastern entrance is the Mahadwaram. The centre of the temple complex consists of an enclosure below the level of the principal gates of the cardinals. This enclosure has Salamandapas at the northern and southern sides. In the inner court yard there are Nandimandapa, Veerasiromandapa, the temple of Mallikarjuna, the temple of Bhramaramba. These are all in a row from east to west. Besides, there are some minor shrines as well in the complex.

After our long walk through the fenced path we were exposed to an open large sized pillared Nandimandapa. Square shape Mandapa had porches projected to the three sides and had 42 pillars. Some pillars were having ornate designing. The raised Adhistana there had two compartments. In the raised central portion a huge Nandi (Divine bull) was seated facing the shrine of Mallikarjuna. The central portion of the ceiling had the figure of Siva and Parvati riding on the bull. The sculpting of Dikpalas on the ceiling was said to be a rare feature.

We walked past the Nandimandapa and reached the structure known as Veerasiromandapa. This open Mandapa with 16 pillars was said to have been built by the Reddy King Anavema Reddy in the year 1378 AD. According to the inscription the original Mandapa had 38 pillared structures with a spacious central hall possessing arched Torans and flanked by Dwarapalakas image. But most of these were seen disfigured and in ruined state.

Finally we reach the main temple of Lord Mallikarjuna, which was situated in the centre of inner courtyard and faced to the east. This temple consisted of Mukhamandapa, Antarala and Garbhagriha. We were still following the queue.

Mukhamandapa situated to the west of the Veerasiromandapa was an elaborated closed hall consisting of 16 pillars. This Mandapa was also named as Mahamandapa. It is said to have been built by the Vijayanagara king, Harihararaya – II in the year 1405 AD. There were three entrance gates with pillared porches on the east, south and north. At the south – west of this Mandapa there was four handed seated Vinayaka made of fine red stone and named as Ratnagarbha Ganapathi. In the north – west, there were placed forty handed Veerabhadra holded with various weapons and four handed Bhadrakali both made with black stone and are in standing posture. We stood before the east opening of this Mandapa where a Nandi of black stone faces to the self emanated Jyothirlinga of Mallikarjuna.

We could see a simple and plain structure known as Antharala, which had a two pillared entrance like structure. The front portions of the pillars were decorated with a silver covering having Dwarapalakas on both sides.

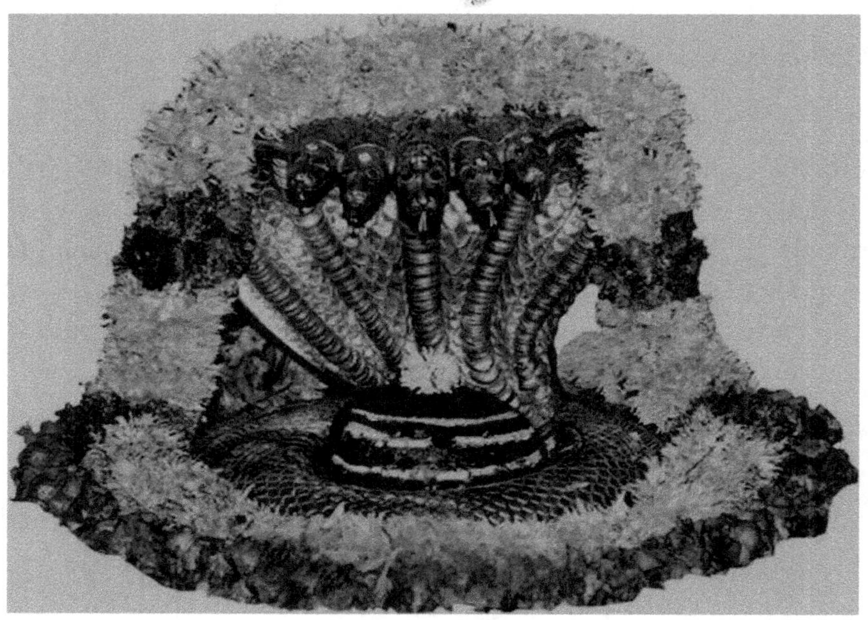

Lord Mallikarjuna Mahadev Jyotirlingam

Antharala leads to Garbhagriha through the ornamental entrance. On the lower horizontal jamb, a purnakumba along with a female deity holding a lotus bud was seen where as on the top Gajalakshmi was shown. On the two vertical jambs, foliage was very artistically depicted. At the centre of the structure was located the self emanated Jothirlinga on a Panavattam. This Panavattam was told to be a latter addition around the Shivalinga which is about a foot in height. The interior portion of the Sikhara of the Sanctum Sanctorum was simple without any artistic decorations. We stood bowed our head for a while before the Lord Mallikarjuna Mahadev and offered our reverence and prayers. A distance had kept the devotees away from the Shivalinga. We tried to stand for a while but the rush from the rear did not allow us to do so.

We came out of the Jyotirling shrine and started a parikrama. From outside we looked at the temple top. It is in the form of a stepped gold plated pyramidal structure. It has nine tiers in reducing dimension from bottom to the top. All sides of the tiers are joined at central portion with Simhalalata sculptures. Below the pinnacle, on all four sides, four Nandi sculptures were seen. The purnakumba on the top is seating on an eight pettalled lotus.

It goes back to ancient times. The Puranas and other literary works spoke about the glory antiquity of Shrisailam. The Nasik inscription of Queen Naganika of the Satavahana dynasty mentioned Sirithana. This is identified with Srisailam. The earliest inscription found at Srisailam belonged sixth century A.D. This confirmed Srisailam as the place known as a Siddhakshetra. The Harsha Charita of a same period also termed Srisailam as a Siddhakshetra.

The first historically significant inscription found at Srisailam belongs to Pradaba Rudra of 1313 A.D. Based on those further research concluded that the early Srisailam temple might have been constructed during the first century A.D. or prior to it.

Mythology however leads to a common belief that this Holy Kshetram exists from time immemorial. The Agni Puranam, in the Krithayuga mentioned that the Demon King Hiranyakasyapa did penance at this place. Being his Puja Mandiram and Ahobila Kshetram he worshipped God Mallikarjuna Swamy here. The Skanda Purana proclaims that in the Trethayuga Lord Sri Rama with Seetha Devi during their banishment has visited this Kshetram and consecrated Sahasra Lingas here. The Epic literatures clear that in the Dwapara Yuga, Arjuna during his pilgrimage and the Pandavas during their exile spent some time in this Kshetram. Even now there is a pond at the foot way of Srisailam called as Bheemuni Kolanu. It is also said that Bhagavan Dattatreya did penance at this Kshetram. Even today there is a tree (Sthala Vriksham) in the temple complex named a Dattatreya Vriksham. In the Kaliyuga the Advaitha Philosopher Adisankara, Siddha Nagarjuna, Veerasaiva Saint Allama Prabhu, Sivasarani Akka Mahadevi spent some time at this Kshetram and worshipped the deities.

There are many Legends associated with Lord Mallikarjuna Mahadev in Srisailam. Among these the most significant are the stories of Parvatha, Arunasura, Chandravati, Vasumathi and Vriddha Mallikarjuna. Parvatha story goes as follows: Parvatha, son of Silada Maharshi is said to have performed penance, pleased Siva and made him agree to live on his body. He also prayed Siva that all the Devathas and sacred waters of all theerthas permanently remain on his top and all the Devotees irrespective of cast or creed visiting the scared place should be blessed with the Moksha. God Siva granted these desires of Parvatha. The Parvatha assumed the shape big Hill 'Srisailam' and Shiva lived on its top as Sriparvatha Swamy.

Story of Arunasura goes as follows: According to Hindu Mythology, Goddess Adisakthi acquired the shape of Bhramaram (bee) to kill the cruel demon Arunasura and afterward settled at Srisailam as Bhramaramba Devi. It is said that here the neck portion of Sati Devi was fallen and hence this place has became as Sakthi Pith.

Story of Chandravati goes as follows: Chandravati was a princess. Once she decided to do penance and meditation. She chose Kadali Vana for this purpose. One day she witnessed a miracle. A Kapila cow was standing under a Bilwa tree and milk was flowing from all of its four udders, sinking into the ground. The cow kept doing this as a routine chore every day. Chandravati dug up that area and was dumb founded at what she saw. There was a self-raising Swyambhu Shiva Linga. It was bright and shining like the Sun rays, and looked like it was burning, throwing flames in all directions. Chandravati prayed to Shiva in this Jyotirlinga. She built a huge Shiva Temple there. Lord Shankara was very pleased with her. Chandravati went to Kailash wind borne. She received salvation and Mukti. On one of the stone-inscriptions of the temple, Chandravati's story can be seen carved out.

Vriddha Mallikarjuna story goes as follows: Once there lived a princess. She was a staunch devotee of Lord Shiva. Pursuing her devotion through continuous worshipping she wished to marry him. One night in dream Siva told her to follow a black bee and stayed where it settled till his arrival. She woke up from dream, found a bee, followed it and reached the mountain of Srisailam. The bee finally settled on a jasmine shrub and princes waited there. She did penance for Shiva for several days and months. Meanwhile the Chenchu tribal nourished her with honey and forest fruits every day. At last Shiva appeared before her with his old and wrinkled face. He said that in search of her he became old. The princess married him. On the occasion of marriage the Chenchus invited the couple for dinner and offered meat and drink. Shiva did not accept that meal. The princess insisted him. At last Shiva left the spot and went away. The princes called him for several times. But he did not listen to her. Then she cursed him to become a stone (Linga). He became Vriddha Mallikarjuna Swamy. On observing this, Parvathi cursed her to become Bhramaram (bee) as she followed him. Even now in the temple complex of Srisailam there is the Shrine of Vriddha Mallikarjuna. Some Scholars opined that the Vriddha Mallikarjuna Linga is probably a fossil of Arjuna Vriksham. They concluded that this was the oldest structure in the entire complex of Srisailam and is of 70 to 80 thousand years old approximately.

Story of Chenchu Mallayya goes as follows: The local tribes Chenchus state that on one occasion Shiva came to Srisailam forest as a hunter. He fell in love with a Chenchu girl, married her and settled down on the hill. Based on this story they look upon Mallikarjuna Swamy as their relation and call him as Chenchu Mallayya. This story is also seen depicted on the Prakaram wall of the temple.

After offering our prayers to Lord Mallikarjuna Mahadev we came out of the temple and took a round of the surrounding site. We stood in a queue which leads us to adjacent temple complex of goddess Bhramaramba Dev. It is one of the Holi Ashthadasha Shakti Peethas. It is believed that upper lip part of Sati Devi's corpse had fallen here. This is the temple of Devi Sati where she is worshipped as Bhramaramba Devi and is considered as a very ferocious deity. Originally she was worshipped by the local tribes Chenchu people.

As we were not allowed to carry cameras/ mobiles we could not take any photographs of the inside of the temple. Only a few scan copies of the photographs of the Garvgriha as available from the printed books are provided here for readers' perusal. We could take the photograph of the Bhramaramba Devi temple from outside.

We went back to our hotel to complete our breakfast. We then started our sightseeing around Srisailam. We visited the important places of pilgrimage interests viz. Sakhshi Ganapati, Hatkeshwara Mahadev, Paldhara panchadhara and Shikharam. Visit to Sakshi Ganapati temple made Lord Ganesh as the witness of our visit to Lord Mallikarjuna Mahadev. Hatkeshwara Mahadev temple situated on the hill is considered geologically very important. Ancient historical evidences were found at this place, which later corroborated about Srisailam existence. Paldhara panchadhara is said to be the place which was visited by Great Sage Adi Sankaracharya. He stayed at here for sometimes and worshiped Lord Shiva. Shikharam is the highest point of the Sriparvatha from where we could see the entire Shrisailam town below.

After completing this tour we went for Ropeway riding and Patalgamga darshan. Ropeway brought us down on the bank of the Krishna River. The place was beautiful. A major dam was built in there on the River Krishna. Patalganga is the local name of the river Krishna which is flowing about 1000 ft below the Srisailam town. Boat ride took us close to the Srisailam Dam. A huge reservoir named Neelam Sanjeeva Reddy Sagar was formed by the surrounding hills. The scenic beauty of the place refreshed us. We sat on the steps of the Patalganga Ghat and spent sometimes playing with the fishes of the Krishna River which touched our feet. These steps were built by Rani Ahilyabai Holker. We rode back through ropeway to hill top and then returned to Hotel for comforting our tired body.

Srisailam was a small hilly place. We do not know how and why we visited this remote place. Lord Shiva perhaps made our connection. Trip to Srisailam would remain in our memory for long time. Memorable Srisailam is God's own place amidst nature.

Lord Mallikarjuna Mahadev's eternal blessings are seen amongst the local tribes. He has lapped the place with all its kindness. Touch of Lord's kindness has been felt in the simplicity of the tribal life there. However materialistic undesired development is slowly tilting the ecological balance towards decay of its natural environment. The taste of the laddoo which we bought as Prasad from the temple is still lingering in our mouth as if we have just eaten. Yes I still miss the Prasadam.

Chapter Twenty Two

Bowing before Sevak Lord Baidyanath

Greatest Bengali Poet Nobel Laureate Tagore had once written -

"Bahu din dhare, bahu croshe ghure, Bahu byay kare, bahu desh ghure (For many days together, covering many miles, spending a lot of money, in travelling many countries)

Dekhite giyechhi parbatmala, dekhite giyechhi Sindhu (To see the mountains, to see the oceans)

Dekha hoinai chankkhu melia (Never watched through my open eyes)

 Ghar hoite dui pa felia (From my home two steps away),

Ekti dhaner shisher upar ekti sisirbindu" (the beauty of a dew drop on a sheaf of paddy tip)

Getting translated in English these summaries "I have seen many places all over the world but I have not seen the beauty of a dew drop on the sheaf of paddy tip near my house".

I have been to ten of the twelve Jyotirlingas which are located far from my native place and in the far flung difficult places in my country. But I am yet to see the one which is relatively near to my home state Bengal. I am talking about our intention to visit Lord Baidyanath Dham situated in Deoghar in the Santhal Parganas division of the state of Jharkhand. Deoghar is surrounded by Dumka, Rajmahal and Bhagalpur in the North-East, by Munger in the North-West, by Hazaribag in the West and by Giridih district in the South.

Last March we planned to visit Lord Baidyanath Mahadev Jyotirlinga. We travelled by Duronto Exp from Howrah and reached Jasidih mid-afternoon. From there we took auto to reach Deoghar which was at a distance of just 7 km. We checked into the Jharkhand Govt tourist hotel where we had booked our room well in advance. Hotel appeared to be well maintained. My wife ordered some quick snacks while I enquired from the reception about Jyotirling Shrine Darshan and local sightseeing. Accordingly we fixed a local cab for next day for whole day sightseeing. After the lunch we took some rest. In the evening we visited the Jyotirling Shrine as it was situated close by our hotel. Fortunately it was the time of Sandhya Aarti (Evening Puja) and we enjoyed the sight through Large TV Monitor put outside the temple hall.

Next morning we started early and straightway reached the Jyotirlinga Shrine. Our priest was waiting for us there. After parking our shoes, etc in a place known by the priest we proceeded to the temple barefooted. We walked through the narrow road having shops on both sides selling various puja articles, etc. Then we passed through the narrow famous pedawala lane to the western side main gate of the temple. The temple complex was a huge area. The Baba Baidyanath temple complex consisted of the main temple of Baba Baidyanath, where the Jyotirlingam was self-emitted and 21 other temples. The layout below will give an idea of how these 22 temples are laid out inside the campus.

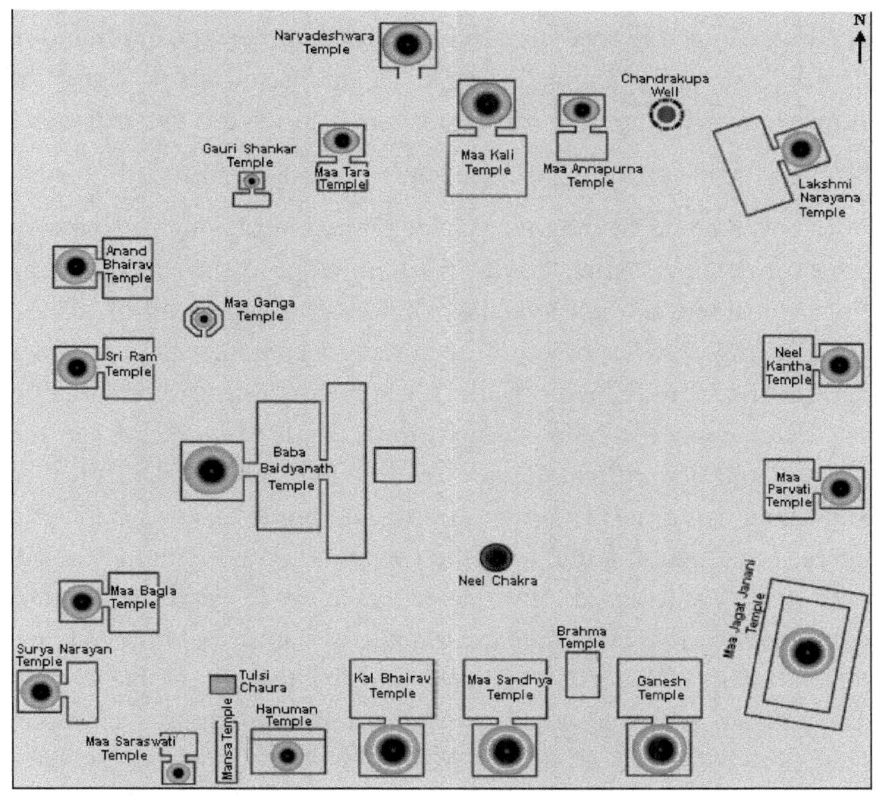

(Source: Baidyanath Dham, Deoghar)

The temple of Lord Baidyanath or Shiva faces the east. It was of a plain stone structure with a pyramidal tower, 72 feet tall as it is said. According to religious belief this temple was built by God Vishwakarma, the Architect of Gods. We entered through the temple main entrance, passed through the middle part and reached the portico (veranda) which leads to the Garbha Griha (Sanctum Sanctorum). In front of the Garbha Griha the veranda had several pillars spanned by blocks of basalt and there was a sandstone image of Nandi on one side. There were bells fixed in the ceiling. Pilgrims pull the bell ropes to announce their approach to the divinity. Through the northern verandah offered flower with water and milk flowed in to a large masonry vat. The composite liquid in it was essentially a mix of milk, sandal paste and washing of flowers, which imparted a fragrant smell to it and was treated as highly sacred.

We stood in the queue which was long enough to take an hour for darshan. After the due time we reached the sanctum. The lingam inside was rarely visible. There was a quite a bit of rush in the morning. People forcefully vied with one another to pour water and see the sacred Shiva lingam. We somehow managed to hold on our place with the help of our Priest Panda. We could see the Lingam and poured our flowers, revered bel (bilvashtakam) leaves and sacred water of the Ganges on it. The priest took my hand and enabled me touching the tip of the Lingam. Likewise he did for my wife too. We offered our prayer. Instantly a great feeling of overwhelmedness ran inside us. It made us happy and relieved. We thanked Lord for not letting trod upon by the aggressive crowd. The Lingam is said to be of cylindrical form and about 5 inches in diameter. It is said to have remained projected out of the base about 4 inches from the centre of a large slab of basalt. We could not see the base of the Lingam as it was fully covered with flowers and Bilva leaves below there. It was not possible to ascertain how much of the lingam is buried. The top was seen broken and had uneven surface.

It was a pitiable sight to see so many people waiting for hours and hours just to get a momentary darshan of the Lord. The crowd should be regulated for darshan in controlled manner to avoid this type of situation. Crowd control is better in all other Jyotirlinga Shrines. This indiscipline among the mass pilgrims and crowd maniac is found more as you proceed towards east in the country.

After our Darshan of Lord Shiva, we came out of the Jyotirlinga Shrine. We stood on the temple complex to look around. The main temple looked as if beyond historical dates. It is said that Lord Rama, the king of Ayodhya visited this temple in the Treta Yuga. The temple top contained three ascending shaped gold vessels that were compactly set. They were donated by the Maharaja of Giddhaur Raja Puran Singh. Besides these pitcher shaped vessels, there was a Punchsula (Five knives in Trident shape), which is considered as rare and only seen in this Shiva Jyotirling Shrine. In the inner top there is an eight pettalled lotus jewel called Chandrakanta Mani.

The courtyard had eleven other temples. Among them main temples were of Goddess Parvathi, Goddess Kali, Goddess Jagat Janani, Kal Bhairav and Lakshminarayan. Goddess Parvathi temple was seen tied up with the main temple with huge red sacred threads which was unique and worthy of reverence showing the unity of Shiva and Shakti.

The legends associated with the origin of the Jyotirlingam and the Shiva temple was many. One legend, according to *Shiva Purana* has it that in the Treta Yuga the demon Ravana, King of Lanka (Srilanka), propitiated Lord Mahadeva and wanted him to come over to Lanka to make his capital invincible. Mahadeva did not agree to his prayer. Proud Ravana attempted to lift Mount Kailash and take it with him to his capital. However Lord Shiva crushed it with his finger. Ravana sought mercy for his arrogance. Lord Shiva told Ravana that one of the twelve emblems of his divinity, Jyotirlinga, would be quite as effective as his presence. He might take it away on the condition that there should be no break in the journey back to Lanka and the lingam would never be placed anywhere on the earth. If the lingam was put anywhere on the earth in the course of the journey, it would get fixed to that spot forever. The legend was that Ravana agreed to this condition and took the lingam and started his journey back to Lanka happily. All the Gods feared the effect of the lingam being established at the seat of the demon king. Ravana would become invincible and his evil and anti-Vedic deeds would threaten the world. They never liked to see Lord Shiva as his protector. They objected to this plan.

They devised a plan for outwitting Ravana. God Varuna, the god of the waters entered the stomach of Ravana. Ravana had to descend to earth to relieve him. Meanwhile Lord Ganesh in the garb of an old Brahmin appeared before Ravana after his descent to the earth and began to converse with him. Unaware of the trick Ravana requested the Brahmin to hold the Jyotirlinga for a few minutes so that he could relieve himself. Lord Ganesh readily agreed to it. Unfortunately Ravana could not ease himself soon. After waiting for long enough Lord Ganesh meanwhile placed the Jyotirlinga on the spot and vanished. This place is known as Baidyanath Dham. When Ravana came back, he found that the Jyotirlinga was firmly fixed to the earth. Ravana tried hard to remove the lingam from the spot where it had been placed. He could not turn out the lingam even an inch. This made him frustrated and realized that a trick had been played on him. Out of frustration, he used violence and pressed it with his thumb so it went inside and got tilted slightly. The Lingam got damaged in the process. Later on he felt guilty of his doings and begged for forgiveness. However, failing to remove the lingam, he made his obeisance to the lingam. Daily he used to come from Lanka and worship the divinity. The spot where Ravana came down to the earth has been identified with Harila Jori, about 6 km north of

Babadham. The place where the lingam was deposited has become famous as Babadham.

According to other traditions, the Linga which was placed by Lord Ganesh in the guise of a Brahmin lay neglected after the death of Ravana until it was noticed by a rude hunter Baiju. He accepted it as his God and worshiped it daily. He proclaimed it to the world as the Lord of Baiju (from where the name migrated to become as Baidyanath).

Another legend has it that according to Hindu beliefs, the demon king Ravana worshipped Shiva at the current site of the temple to get the boons that he later used to wreak havoc in the world. Ravana offered his ten heads one after another to Shiva as a sacrifice. Pleased with this, Lord Shiva descended to cure Ravana who was injured. As Lord Mahadev acted as a doctor, he is referred to as Baidya ("doctor"). Hence forth this Form of appearance of Lord Shiva becomes known as Lord Baidyanath and the temple as the Baidyanath Dham.

We walked around in the complex and reached near a Tank. It is believed by the Hindus that this tank was the same tank where Lord Ganesh after taking the lingam from Ravana consecrated it in dew form with water. This tank is known as Shivaganga today. However Legend also has that King Ravana was supposed to have excavated a well with an arrow and brought into it the waters of all the sacred pools of the earth. This well is known as Chandrakoopa today.

We also came to know that this place Baidyanath Dham was one of the 51 Shaktipeeths. According to the Hindu belief the heart of Sati fell at Babadham. Hence this place is also known as Hridayapeeth or Hardapeeth. Although there is no separate shrine for Shaktipeeth here to commemorate this occurrence, there is a temple of Goddess Parvati on the eastern side of the complex. The temple has high base and stands facing the Jyotirling shrine. We climbed the stairs to access the temple. It contained two idols made of stone – one of Goddess Parvati on the left and the other Goddess Durga on the right. There was also rushing of worshippers to offer prayer. We could complete our Darshan relatively quickly with the help of our Panda.

In the past some confusion raised about the exact place of the Baidyanath Jyotirling Shrine. People were confused Parli located in the western India as the location. But in the Sivmahapuran Kotirudra Samhita and Sivmahapuran Satarudra Samhita ancient verses identified the location of Baidyanath Jyotirling was in 'Chidabhoomi'. Chidabhoomi was the ancient name of Deoghar. In Dwadasa Jyothirlinga Sthothram (slokas), Adi Sankaracharya has praised Baidyanath Jyothirlinga in following verses:

"Poorvothare prajwalika nidhane
sada vasantham girija sametham
surasuraradhitha padapadmam
srivaidyanatham thamaham namami"

As per this Baidyanath Jyotirling was located at Prajwalika nidhanam (meaning funeral place i.e., Chithabhoomi) in the North-Eastern part of the country. Deoghar is far located in east. This is in absolute contradiction to the place Parli which is in west central part of the country. Further Chidabhoomi indicated that in olden days this was a funeral place. This place could have been a center of tantric cults like Kapalika/Bhairava where Lord Shiva is worshipped. Bhavishyapurana also narrated the existence of Baidyanath. It referred to the tract comprising the present district and Birbhoom as Narikhand. It has described the location as "situated west of the Dwarikashwari River and extending along the Panchakuta hills on its west, and approaches Kikta on the north". This description matches very accurately with the place of Deoghar.

Various manuscripts and inscriptions suggest that the history of the Babadham or the Baidyanath Dham goes back to the period of the 8th century A.D. The region was then ruled by the last Gupta Emperor Adityasena Gupta. The Babadham temple has been famous since then. As mentioned in the *Aine - Akbari* of Mughal Emperor Akbar one of his confident Raja Man Singh was attached to the Giddhaur dynasty of this region for a long time. Man Singh's brother, Bhan Singh was married to daughter of Puran Mal, the 9th descent of the Giddhaur dynasty. Man Singh had great faith in this Shrine and got a tank "Mansarovar" excavated. Puran Mal's inscription proves his connection with the Babadham temple. An inscription on the stone wall near the Garvgriha door in the central sanctum of Baidyanath temple states that he built it in 1516 AD at the request of the priest Raghunath Ojha. After the death of Puran Mal, the priest had a new porch created as per an oracle of Lord Shiva. He set his own inscription therein and claimed the credit of having created the entire temple.

Khulasati-t-twarikh written in the Muslim period between 1695 and 1699 A.D, also confirmed about the pilgrimage to Baidyanath Dham. In the 18th century under the Mughal rule the temple administration had to part a fixed rent with them. The then Maharaja of Giddhaur did not like that. After a fight with the Mughal authority he brought back Babadham under his rule. Subsequently the British East India Company took over the management from 1757 AD onwards. However later British administrator withdraw their policy of interference and handed over the control of the temple to the High Priest.

Baidyanath Dham or Babadham as locally known is one of the 12 important Shiva Jyotirlingas. The temple is only one of its kinds in the eastern India. A visit to this temple and seeing the maddening crowds will rekindle our thinking about the enormous belief in Lord Shiva the people have. A glance of the Baidyanath Jyotirling would alone free human from the rebirth-death cycle. The Swayambhu Linga had emerged from the place where Devi Sati's heart was fallen. This fact had this place most significantly associated with Hindu spiritualism and religious practices. Our visit to Lord Baidyanath Mahadev at Deoghar was wonderful and unforgettable. We spent a memorable time in moving around Deoghar (used to be one of my childhood fantasies) for sightseeing of the places surrounding the Baidyanath Dham.

Chapter Twenty Three

End of Human Pain before Lord Kedarnath

Hindus believe Lord Mahadev resides in Mount Kailash. It is situated on the Himalaya Mountain range in the northern border. It is protecting our country from both natural calamity and foreign enemies. High altitude seat of Lord Kedarnath ensure that his Bhaktas or Disciples undergo a determined pursue to reach him as if it constitute the great penance. Once His disciple is before him it becomes his responsibility to remove all their pains. Seating at the Kedarnath mountain range Lord Kedarnath is thus regarded amongst the Hindus the most revered of the twelve Jyotirlingas.

That was the time when we were staying at Kanpur. We planned our visit to Kedarnath in mid-October. After deciding the travel route we completed related bookings and other paraphernalia. We reached Haridwar by Sangam Express and straightway proceeded to Rishikesh to check in to our reserved hotel. After refreshing ourselves we had our launch. Then with the hotel people we fixed our Taxi for Guptkashi for next morning. We were informed that our travel would cover Devprayag, Srinagar, and Rudraprayag to reach Guptkashi. We were told that our route would cover as follows: Rishikesh-Devprayag (75 km, 2.5 hrs) - Srinagar (40 km, 1.5 hrs) – Rudraprayag (34 km, 1 hr) – Guptkashi (48 km, 1.5 hr). We preferred taxi as we could travel at our will and stop anywhere we like on our way.

After travelling for over 2 hrs on the beautiful scenic road we arrived at Devprayag. Devprayag is the first of the Panch Prayag. We saw the confluence of the Bhagirathi and the

Alaknanda. We took a few photographs of this beautiful holy world. After spending sometimes we started for Srinagar. We reached there in about an hour. Srinagar is one of the nice picturesque green valleys of Uttarakhand. We took a few photographs. We spent about 20 mins and then restarted. After travelling for about an hour through the ups and down of the hilly tract we reached Rudraprayag. Here we saw the famous confluence of the two rivers - the Mandakini and the Alaknanda. Rudraprayag, the second among the Panch Prayag has the rugged beauty created by the tall hills surrounding from all sides. Spending sometimes we then started for Guptkashi. The route from here to Guptkashi was extremely scenic. The altitude was also changing and the road was uneven at places and appeared a bit risky too. We crossed places viz, Tilwara, Augustamuni and Kund before reaching Guptakashi. Thoroughly soaked in the scenic beauty of the holy land we finally reached Guptkashi at around 1PM. We straightway checked into our reserved hotel. On the way we had seen the Guptkashi Helipad. We got freshened up and had light refreshment. We collected necessary information related to next day's Helicopter flight from the hotel people.

We reached Guptakashi helipad early in the next morning wearing adequate warm clothing. We carried in a small shoulder bag some medicines and a water bottle beside the camera. Our helicopter took off on schedule time. The weather was good. Helicopter reached a great height. High peaks of Himalayan mountain range were clearly visible. We thought had we not had this Helicopter trip we would have missed life's greatest natural views. Helicopter flew us over the Mandakini valley. The sky over this valley is infamous for being filled with frequent clouds causing incessant rains. Such happenings normally disrupt the helicopter flights.

Soon we were delighted to see the top of the Temple of Lord Kedarnath. The full view of the Kedarnath Temple in the backdrop of the snow-clad peaks came in to our notice. Our helicopter gradually approached the helipad of Kedarnath. Upon arrival the helipad staff greeted us and helped us to get down from the helicopter. We were given one and half to 2 hrs time for visiting Lord Kedarnath temple. The person was kind enough to caution us that we should walk slowly as there may be issue of sudden exposure to high altitude sickness due to less oxygen.

The Temple was about 500 meters away from the helipad. We climbed some stairs on the way. In the company of one staff we moved towards the holy shrine of Lord Kedarnath. On the way, we bought flowers and Prasadam from the makeshift shops for offering to Lord Kedarnath. We had to search for Bilvapatra and finally got from one shop. We felt a sudden drop in the temperature but it did not bother us as we were prepared for this.

As we approached the temple I managed to take a few shots of the temple from distance keeping the snowy mountain peaks in the backdrop. The long shot view was majestic.

This temple place is at an altitude of 11755 ft in the Mandakini valley. I felt that in the form of tall snow clad mountain peaks nature has protected the temple from all sides. These surroundings dipped the place in heavenly peace and tranquility. The positive vibe of the place made me feel within my soul "this is really the Home of Gods'. We wondered how the temple of this magnitude could be built in such a seclude place like this more than 1000 years ago, which appeared to be so difficult to reach by human being even today.

We were fortunate enough that so far there was no weather disruption. The crowd present there was also manageable. We followed a small queue and had our darshan after a short wait. We passed by the Nandi who seated in front of the temple after ascending through the large gray steps leading to the holy sanctums. We found inscriptions said to be in Pali on the steps. We entered the temple.

The first hall was a small pillared hall in front of the temple containing statues of the Goddess Parvathi and of the five Pandava brothers, Lord Krishna, Nandi, the vehicle of Shiva and Virabhadra, one of the greatest guards of Shiva. Statue of Draupadi and other deities are also seen installed in the main hall.

Then we proceeded to inner hall, containing the sanctum sanctorum where the Jyotirlinga was housed. We found the lingam of Lord Kedarnath. Unlike its usual ovoid form, this was pyramidal. The Lingam was of irregular shape with a pedestal 12 ft in circumference and 12 ft in height. This was regarded as one of the 12 Jyotirlings. We offered our prayer with bowed heads. We were also allowed to touch the triangular Jyotirlinga by the priest. We felt the divine energy did engulf us for a while. We spent some peaceful moments inside the temple totally aloof from the outside world. These were such moments we did not feel earlier anywhere else. We came out of the temple fully drenched with the Graces and Blessings of Lord Kedarnath. A feeling of unsatiety however mixed with curiosity was killing me from inside. But we had to end our darshan and come out of the temple.

Photography was not allowed inside the temple. So a scan picture of the Lord Kedarnath is shown here. The Spire of the Kedarnath temple looked great with the Kedarnath Mountain in the background. This temple was an impressive stone edifice of unknown date, possibly over a few thousand years old. It was built of massive stone slabs over a large rectangular platform. The structure is believed to have been constructed in the 8th century AD, when Adi Shankaracharya visited this place. He was believed to have revived the temple to the present structure.

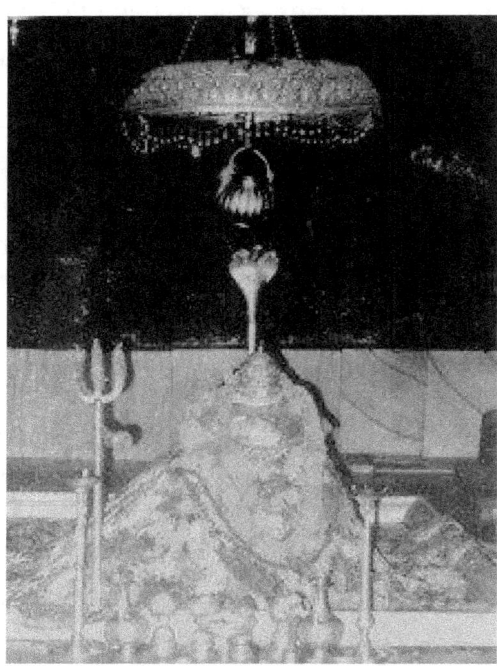

Kedarnath Jyotirlinga

Earlier this temple was on a site adjacent to where Pandavas were believed to have built the original temple. The origin of the revered temple can be found in the great epic – Mahabharata. This ancient temple had undergone many renovations regularly over the centuries.

There are many legends associated with this great Jyotirling shrine. One Legend goes that Nara and Narayana – two incarnations of Vishnu once performed severe penance in front of a Shiva lingam made out of earth in Badrikashraya of Bharat Khand. Pleased with their devotion, Lord Shiva appeared in front of them and said that they might ask for a boon. Nar and Narayan requested Shiva to take up a permanent abode as a Jyotirlingam at Kedarnath so that all people who worship Lord Shiva shall be freed from their miseries. Lord Shiva agreed and the lingam became famous as Kedarnath Jyotirlinga.

The popularly-narrated legend goes as follows: Subsequent to the Kurukshetra war the Pandavas were feeling guilty of having killed their own relatives. God Krishna advised them to seek pardon from Lord Shiva to atone for their sins of fratricide and Brahmanhatya, committed by them during the war. They should pray for his blessings before attaining salvation and to seek blessings for Moksha. After handing over the Kingdom to their sons and grandsons the Pandavas went for a pilgrimage. But Lord Vishveshwar was away in Mount Kailash in the Himalayas. Keeping in mind the advices of Lord Krishna the Pandavas left Kashi and reached the Himalayas via Haridwar.

Lord Shiva knew that Pandavas were planning to seek his pardon. But Shiva hid from them as he was not willing to meet them since he was annoyed with them for the unjust events of the war. He therefore, avoided meeting them at Kashi. He went incognito as the bull Nandi from there to Guptakashi. One of the Pandavas happened to see Him from a distance at Rudraprayag. Dharmaraj Yudhishtir did lament "Oh, Lord, You have hidden yourself from our sight because we have sinned. But we will seek you (Lord Shiva) out somehow. Only after we take your Darshan would our sins be washed away". This place, where Lord Shiva had hidden himself became known as Guptkashi and became a famous shrine. From Guptakashi (Dist. Rudraprayag), the Pandavas wandered in the Himalayas in search of Lord Shiva and reached a place later known as Gaurikund in the Himalayan valleys. They wandered there in search of Lord. While doing so Nakul and Sahadev two younger Pandavas found a Buffalo. It was unique to look at. Then Bheema went after the buffalo with his mace. The buffalo was clever and Bheema could not catch it. But Bheema managed to hit the buffalo with his mace. The buffalo had its face hidden in a crevice-in the earth in a cave like place in the midst of Mandakini valley near Chorabali glacier. The place was known as Kedar. Bheema started to pull the buffalo by its tail. In this tug-of war the face of the buffalo went straight to Nepal, leaving its hind part in Kedar. The face of the buffalo later became known as Pashupatinath in Nepal.

When the Buffalo dived in to the ground in an attempt to hide and escape from Bhima, Bhima put his might to pull out the bull but failed. Only the hind with the hump left out of the earth and rest parts vanished into the ground. This portion appeared to have taken a triangular rock shape as depicted in the stone form and the hump has taken the form of present day Shiva Linga. On this hind part of Buffalo a glorious Jyotirlinga appeared. Lord Shankara appeared from this great light before the Pandavas. By getting a Darshan of Lord Shankar, the Pandavas were absolved of their sins. The Lord told the Pandavas, "From now on, I will remain here as a triangular shaped Jyotirlinga. By taking a Darshan of Kedarnath, devotees would attain piety". Thus the Shivalinga become famous as one of the 12 Shiva Jyotirlingas.

Near Kedarnath, there are many symbols of the Pandavas. Raja Pandu died here and the place is famous as Pandukeshwar. The mountain top where the Pandavas went to enter the Swarga is known as "Swargarohini". When Darmaraja was leaving for Swarga, one of his fingers fell on the earth. At that place Dharmaraj installed a Shiva Linga, which is the size of the thumb. It is believed that to catch Mahisharupa Lord Shiva Bheema fought with maces. Bheema was struck with remorse. He did massage Lord Shiva's body with ghee. In memory of this event, even today, this triangular Shiva Jyotirlinga is massaged with ghee. Shankara is worshipped here in this manner. Water and Bel leaves are used for Puja worship.

Legend further extended to say that other parts of the Buffalo form of Shiva reappeared in five different places in five different forms namely hump at Kedarnath, face at Rudranath, arms at Tungnath, navel and stomach at Madhyamaheshwar and the locks at Kalpeshwar. Each of these five places came to be collectively known as the Panch Kedars. All these lie in the Garwal Himalayas in the present day state of Uttarakhand.

History of Kedarnath goes as follows: Excavations revealed that it was once the part of the Mauryan Empire as mentioned in the 7th-century travelogue of Huen Tsang. During 8th century AD Adi Shankaracharya, a Hindu spiritual reformer visited the snow-laden heights of Garhwal and established a math named Joshimath. He also restored some of the most sacred shrines, including Badrinath and Kedarnath.

The Jyotirlinga at Kedarnath is of immense spiritual significance to Hindus. By visiting Kedareshwar, sorrows do not come even in dreams. By worshipping Kedareshwar, Pandavas got rid of all their sorrows and of their material ties. Devotees (include many criminals, offenders and sinners) have been getting pulled towards these Kshetras due to the highly benevolent divine presence in these abodes. A few sinners even visit several times in their life time, guided by the belief that Lord would free them from their past sins.

We came out of the Shrine and had quick refreshment before we embarked upon local sightseeing. We visited the Samadhi Mandir of Great Hindu Scholar and Priest Adi Shankaracharya. We are told the famous mountain cliff known as Bhairav Ghati starts little far from the place. There are eight shrines on the eight sides of the temple. We had sometime in hand. So we decided to see the river Mandakini quickly. On our way we visited the Old Shiva temple which is said to have been built by the Pandavas. We reached the bank of the river Mandakini and were overwhelmed. Shortly thereafter we turned to the way to Helipad to catch the waiting helicopter for Guptkashi. Our visit to Lord Kedarnath Shrine was perhaps one of the best acts of our life. Our indomitable desire had taken us to the Lord. We closed our eyes and thank Lord Kedarnath for making our travel comfortable as there was no disruption in the weather. Our return helicopter trip was a bit turbulent as was expected in the Mandakini valley at this time of the day.

After landing at Guptakashi we hired taxi and straightway drove to hotel. On the way we spoke to the driver and lined up with him for sightseeing of Guptakashi. After getting freshened up we had lunch. The waiting taxi took us around the town. Guptakashi, a small hamlet of Rudraprayag district is a holy town.

It is adorned with the many ancient temples and believed to be a part of epic Mahabharata. Located at 47 km from Kedarnath it is situated at an elevation of 4300 ft. We visited two ancient temples Vishwanath temple and Ardhnaarishwar Temple. Vishwanath temple resembles a lot to the Kashi Vishwanath. We saw the Manikarnik Kund in the complex of the Vishwanath temple. The sight of the temple is absolutely captivating. In fact Guptkashi serves as a perfect stopover for those travelling to Kedarnath with its amazing weather, lush green forests and captivating views of Chaukhamba Range.

Taxi then took us to Chopta valley, a Green Heaven. Visiting the valley of Chopta was a life time experience for us. Chopta with minor human adaptation is having mythological spots like the Tungnath Temple and the Deoria Tal. But those can only be accessed by a well guided trek. The Kanchula Korak Musk Deer Sanctuary is located there. We were on the Ukhimath – Gopeswar road, 2 km from Guptkashi city centre. We had a distant glimpse of the Deoria Tal. The lake was surrounded by pine forest. The clear water of the lake was producing the mirror effect of the pines and the distant Chaukhmaba peaks as well.

This small trip had blessed and drenched us with the life-time experience of collating the heavenly giveaways in the form of Himalayan splendour. We were overwhelmed and thanked Lord Mahadeva. We returned to our hotel at Guptkashi before it was dark.

Chapter Twenty Four

The Realisation

Lord Shiva lives in the heart of Hindus through their everyday life. There is nothing in this world which can disengage a Hindu from remembering the Lord. Each day common Hindus worship the divine through a high god or a family deity. To do this they perform puja in a sacred section of the worship room of the home. Puja rituals keep the Hindus aware of their gods and mindful of their duties as individuals. Pujas sustain the power of Belief in God.

The most exalted setting of performing puja is the temple. The temple is the house of God and a link between human existence and the divine. More importantly for Hindu the temple is the place that connects this world with the next. Hindus believe that the temple is not created as a place of God or a place of prayer alone. It is the place of storing energy system too wherein any one can plunge into. Ancient temples of India were built on the basis of great scientific knowledge. If the basic aspects of the temple – the size and shape of the idol, the mudra that the idol holds, the parikrama, the Garbha Griha, and the mantras used to consecrate the idol are properly matched, a powerful energy system is created.

In Indian tradition no one tells us to go to a temple, to worship and to give money and ask for something. Traditionally we believe when we go to the temple, we must sit for a while and come back. We are required to sit there because a field of energy is maintained there. This is a way of recharging ourselves with very positive vibrations of life so that we go back to the world with a different perspective. This important and significant understanding constituted my first realisation about the Jyotirlinga. This is true to any visit to any Temple.

In India Hindus believe that through the idol that they worship energy is manifested in a particular way so that their quality of life can be enhanced. From the standpoint of modern science we know today that everything is the same energy but everything is not the same in the world. This energy can be like an animal or this energy can function like the Divine. The physical body itself can be transformed into a Divine entity if we just reorganize our systems in a particular way. In the Hindu way of life, the important thing in human life is his liberation. Following illustration may clarify further: Between the full moon day and the new moon day each of the fourteen nights are so different. In present time we cannot make the difference between these nights due to the presence of electric light. But if we are left in the open village surrounding where there is no electricity we would realise then every night would be different. The reason being the moon comes up at different times and has different shapes and forms. But it is the same moon. It is not a different entity. The same moon has different impacts at different times i.e. with some rearrangement. Similarly if we re-arrange the energy system in the body which is just a mass of flesh right now, can become a divine entity. The whole system of yoga is oriented towards this. It is from this context we often conclude that many yogis become divine entity whom people worship. It is a reorganized energy – completely engineered is believed to be the source of divinity. In this regard the Hindu belief that Lord Shiva is the greatest Yogi becomes very relevant. This was second most significant understanding.

The Hindu way of life does not entail with "ism" because it is a geographical and cultural identity. Anyone born in the land of Indus is a Hindu. There is no particular belief system, god or ideology which we can call as the Hindu way of life. We can worship a man-god and be a Hindu. We can worship a woman-god and be a Hindu. We can worship a cow and be a Hindu. We can worship a tree and be a Hindu. Or we don't worship anything and we can be a Hindu. Hindu is more a cultural identity, not merely a religious identity. In the Hindu way of life, the only important thing in human life is his liberation. Hindus perceive Lord Shiva through his Omni-presence in his Vishveshwar form motivating mankind for attaining Liberation or Moksha. For Hindus reaching high level of life form Mukti or Liberation becomes the only goal. This constituted my third most significant realisation.

Shiva Temples are specially designed places of worship where the presiding deity is Lord Shiva in the form of a Linga. Linga is an iconic representation of Lord Shiva. In Hindu temples, statues of the deities are present in the sanctum. But in a Shiva temple, only a linga is present. The linga worship is limited only to Lord Shiva, since no other deity is worshipped in linga form. The Shiva Lingam represents the infinite nature of Lord Shiva. My realisation perceives that the linga worship is the symbolic worship of Lord Shiva in a Shiva Temple. In the Puranas like Brahmana Purana, Linga Purana it is said that in the very beginning of creation Lord Shiva appeared before Brahma and Vishnu in the form of a bright splendour endless column of light. Appearance of this linga form of column of bright light forms the basis of the iconic Linga form of Shiva. This account was narrated by the Sage Suta before the other sages when he was asked about the origin of the linga (Ref: Linga Purana). Sage Suta went on to narrate that the endless bright column of light was free from decay and growth constituted the first appearance of Lord Shiva in this Universe. The Linga of the bright column of light was termed as the Jyotirlingam. It is a form of Jyoti. Jyoti is a fire, whose shape is exactly the shape of lingam. Shiva appeared in Jyotirlinga form to solve dispute of Brahma and Vishnu. This constitutes my fourth most important realisation about the Jyotirlinga.

Jyotirlinga carries more significance in term of Shiva's actual form, which is "Nirguna" according to Rigveda and Shiva Maha Purana. Shiva himself gave his introduction to Vishnu and Brahma:

"Gyan Swaroopam Shivohm, Shivohm (Brahma)
Neejanand Swaroopam Shivohm, Shivohm (Vishnu)
Prakash Swaroopam Shivohm, Shivohm (Mahesh- Shiva's 3rd eye)"

On hearing this both Brahma and Vishnu prayed to Shiva to appear so that they could see him. Shiva appeared in Jyotirlingam form, this Jyoti was a fire of love. Twelve Jyotirlingas are 12 Jyotirstambha of Shiva. Shiva is the only deity who is accepted as "Neerakar Nirguna Brahman". Nobody knows the origin of time because nobody exactly existed to check Shiva's origin. So after knowing about Shiva's introduction Vishnu explained that Shiva is actually a seed and whatever we see is a tree originated from that seed, i.e. "Lingam" [Ref: The Mahabharata, Anusasana Parva (Veda Vyasa Mahabharata)]. Vishnu was convinced about the existence of a more powerful entity (Adi Deva or Mahadeva) in the form of Shiva. The blessed Vishnu said: "I salute Mahadeva, salutations to Thee. O Thou that art eternal origin of all things. The Rishis say that Thou art the Lord of the Vedas. The righteous say that Thou art Penance, Thou art Sattwa, Thou art Rajas, Thou art Tamas, and Thou art truth". Vishnu himself said "Shiva is eternal origin. That's why Shiva linga is seed and whatever we see it is just a tree from that seed". It is origin. Shiva is originator. So Shiva is worshiped in the form of Jyotirlingam.

Among the 18 major Maha Puranas, the Linga Purana further glorifies the status of Linga. Linga is worshipped because Linga contains everything of this world. Interfering in the debate of the Sages Goddess Saraswati explained the reason of worshipping the Linga form. She said "the whole world is identical with the Linga. Everything is found on the Linga. Hence, one shall eschew everything, install the Linga and worship it". She continued "all Gods are situated in a Linga. All the deities, Dikpalaks (guardians of the directions), the planets, Ganas, Nandi, Pitras, Rishis, Kuber, Aditya, Samkhya, Aswinikumar- the best of the physicians, Viswadevas, Sadhyas, Pashus, birds and animals, besides all the mobile and immobiles, starting from Brahma are established in the linga. Therefore, leaving aside everything, linga should be consecrated. As every God is situated in Linga it is highly auspicious to worship Linga". She added "Trinities are situated in Linga- Lord Brahma resides at the root, Lord Vishnu in the middle. The lord of all unborn Pashupati in the form of Rudra resides at the top". Thus Goddess Saraswati concluded saying "Sarva Linge Pratisthitam" i.e. "Everything is situated in Linga".

Worship of Lord Shiva in the form of Shivalinga constitutes the most difficult part of one's realisation. I tried to understand the significance of a Jyotirlinga in the life of a Hindu. My realisation is best explained in the following way. The Shivalinga represents the inseparable relation of Shiva and Shakti. The relationship of Uma and Maheswara is like that of word and meaning. The beloved of Shiva (Uma) is in the form of words. The moon crested Lord (Maheswara) is in the form of meaning of those words. Just as meaning is formless and gets manifested through words, similarly formless Shiva gets manifested through Shakti. There is mutual dependence between Shakti and Shiva. There is no Shakti without Shiva and no Shiva without Shakti. The inseparable relationship of Shiva and Shakti was expressed in the form of Ardha Narishwara. However Linga form is the only form which establishes word-meaning relationship. It is believed that formless Shiva gets manifested in Linga form through the base of Shakti. The pedestal of the Linga symbolises Goddess Uma and the Linga is Maheswara himself. Shivalinga therefore represents manifestation of Nirguna in Saguna form. Shivalinga is identical with the Universe itself and it represents infinity too. Thus Shivalinga establishes inseparable relationship of Shiva-Shakti. In short I therefore conclude that worshipping of Linga is highly auspicious as it contains all Gods and Goddesses, as it is identical with the Universe itself, as it represents the Nirguna Brahman, as it represents inseparable relationship of Shiva-Shakti.

All Jyotirlinga Shrines are Shiva Temples but all Shiva temples are not Jyotirlinga Shrines. There is a difference between the two. It is said that Lord Shiva himself is present there at all 12 Jyotirlings where as in temples we do establish a Lord Shiva Murti as an idol or a Shivalinga. Hindus belief no Jyotirlinga is established by human being. It was all already created by Lord Shiva himself with his appearance or incarnation or avatar for fulfilling his benevolent and rescuer act on the earth and was Swyambhu. Human being identified it or discovered it or told about it or blessed with it after realising Lords omnipresence in the Jyotirlinga through its myth and associated legend. My worship was in the form of pilgrimage to Lord Shiva's Jyotirlinga Shrines. This relived my belief in Him. Human Faith stood redefined.

Om Namah Shivaya!

References and Acknowledgment

In my quest to produce a human insight in searching Lord Shiva connection I depended on several sources. Listed below are the books, periodicals, journals, websites resources that I cited to develop the logical base of our mythological and religious faith and belief for my novel. Material was not necessarily used from all of these sources but many of them appeared in one article did open the doors to further research articles. While citing one article only relevant references were collated. Therefore it was not necessary that all such references be read. Relevant information is studied with a view to conceptualise the central theme of the novel I envisaged. I therefore acknowledge all these references and many such advises I received with all humility and respects without which this work would not have been possible.

Books

1. Roshen Dalal (2010). Hinduism: An Alphabetical Guide. Penguin Books. pp. 137, 186.

2. Cush, Robinson &York (2008). Encyclopedia of Hinduism. Routledge. p. 78.

3. K. Sivaraman (1973). Saivism in Philosophical Perspective: A Study of the Formative Concepts, Problems, and Methods of Shaiva Siddhānta. Motilal Banarsidass. p. 131.

4. Jan Gonda (1969), The Hindu Trinity, Anthropos, Bd 63/64, H 1/2, pages 212–226

5. Karen Pechilis Prentiss (2000). The Embodiment of Bhakti. Oxford University Press. p. 199.

6. Tyagi, Ishvar Chandra (1982). Shaivism in Ancient India: From the Earliest Times to 300 A.D. Meenakshi Prakashan. p. 81.

7. Berreman, Gerald Duane (1963). Hindus of the Himalayas. University of California Press. p. 385

8. Klaus K. Klostermaier (2007), A Survey of Hinduism, 3rd Edition, State University of University Press, pp. 24–25,

9. Gregory Maksimovich Bongard-Levin (1985). Ancient Indian Civilization. Arnold-Heinemann. p. 45.

10. Steven Rosen; Graham M. Schweig (2006). Essential Hinduism. Greenwood Publishing Group. p. 45.

11. Namita Gokhale (2009). The Book of Shiva. Penguin Books. pp. 10–11..

12. Stella Kramrisch (1993). The Presence of Siva. Princeton University Press. p. 7.

13. Robert Hume, Shvetashvatara Upanishad, The Thirteen Principal Upanishads, Oxford University Press, pages 399, 403

14. M. Hiriyanna (2000), The Essentials of Indian Philosophy, Motilal Banarsidass, pages 32–36

15. DS Sharma (1990), The Philosophy of Sadhana, State University of New York Press, pages 9–14

16. JS Vasugupta (2012), Siva Sutras, Motilal Banarsidass, pages 252, 259

17. Surendranath Dasgupta (1973). A History of Indian Philosophy. Cambridge University Press. pp. 17, 48–49, 65–67, 155–161.

18. Gavin D. Flood (1996). An Introduction to Hinduism. Cambridge University Press. p. 17.

19. Vasugupta; Jaideva (1979). Siva Sutras. Motilal Banarsidass. pp. xv–xx.

20. James Mallinson (2007). The Shiva Samhita: A Critical Edition. Yoga. pp. xiii–xiv.

21. George Michell (1977). The Hindu Temple: An Introduction to Its Meaning and Forms. University of Chicago Press. pp. 25–26.

22. Lingam: Hindu symbol Encyclopædia Britannica

23. Parrinder, Edward Geoffrey (1982). Avatar and incarnation. Oxford: Oxford University Press. p. 88.

Source References

1. Chakravarti, Mahadev (1986). The Concept of Rudra-Śiva through the Ages (Second Revised Ed.). Delhi: Motilal Banarsidass.
2. Sitansu S. Chakravarti (1991). Hinduism, a Way of Life. Motilal Banarsidass Publ.
3. Chatterjee, J.C. (1986). Kashmir Shaivism. Albany, NY: State University of New York Press.

4. Courtright, Paul B. (1985).Gaṇeśa: Lord of Obstacles, Lord of Beginnings. New York: Oxford University Press.

5. Davis, Richard H. (1992). Ritual in an Oscillating Universe: Worshipping Shiva in Medieval India. Princeton, New Jersey: Princeton University Press.

6. Debnath, Sailen (2009). The Meanings of Hindu Gods, Goddesses and Myths. New Delhi: Rupa & Co.

7. Flood, Gavin (1996). An Introduction to Hinduism. Cambridge: Cambridge University Press.

8. Michaels, Axel (2004). Hinduism: Past and Present. Princeton University Press.

9. Parmeshwaranand, Swami (2004). Encyclopedia of the Śaivism, in three volumes. New Delhi: Sarup & Sons.

10. Radhakrishnan, Sarvapalli (1953), The Principal Upanishads, New Delhi: HarperCollins Publishers India (1994 Reprint),

11. Arvind Sharma (2000). Classical Hindu Thought: An Introduction. Oxford University Press.

Periodicals / Institutional Publications

1. Sri Vishnu Sahasranama, Ramakrishna Math edition, pg.47 and pg. 122.
2. Swami Chinmayananda's translation of Vishnu Sahasranama, p. 24, Central Chinmaya Mission Trust.
3. Singh, S.P., Rigvedic Base of the Pashupati Seal of Mohenjo-Daro (Approx 2500–3000 BC), Puratattva 19: 19–26. 1989
4. Kramrisch, Stella (1981). Manifestations of Shiva. Philadelphia Museum of Art. p. 22.
5. Sivananda, Swami (1996). "Worship of Siva Linga". Lord Siva and His Worship. The Divine Life Trust Society.

6. Swati Mitra (2011). Omkareshwar and Maheshwar. Eicher Goodearth and Madhya Pradesh Government. p. 25.

7. Nath, Vijay (March–April 2001), "From 'Brahmanism' to 'Hinduism': Negotiating the Myth of the Great Tradition", Social Scientist: 19–50,

www.ingramcontent.com/pod-product-compliance
Lightning Source LLC
LaVergne TN
LVHW020750200726
843506LV00009B/969